delicate_
Autumn Fairies

A GOLDEN HUE COLORING ADVENTURE

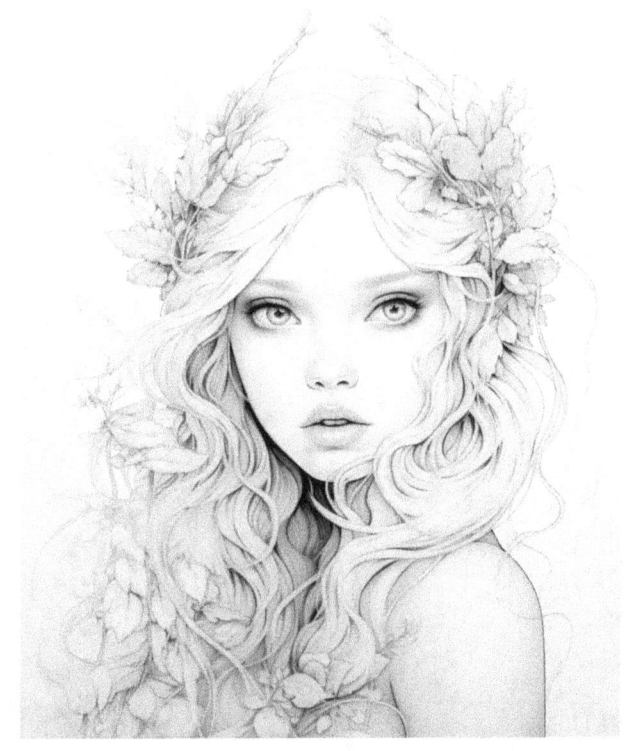

KRISTINA LEWIS

TINY STARS

Publishing :
Tiny Stars Coloring/Kristina Lewis
TinyStarsColoring@yahoo.com

Release date September 2023

Print:
Amazon Distribution

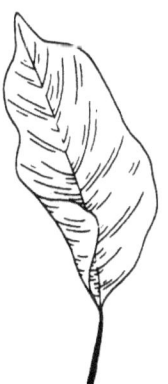

This book belongs to:

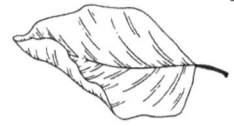

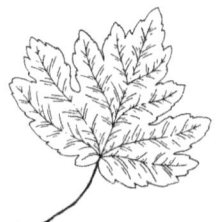

_____

_____

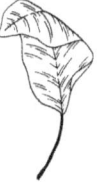

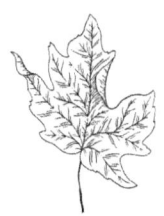

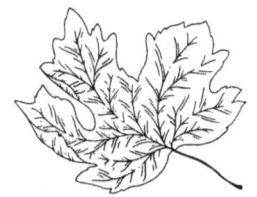

Color Test Page

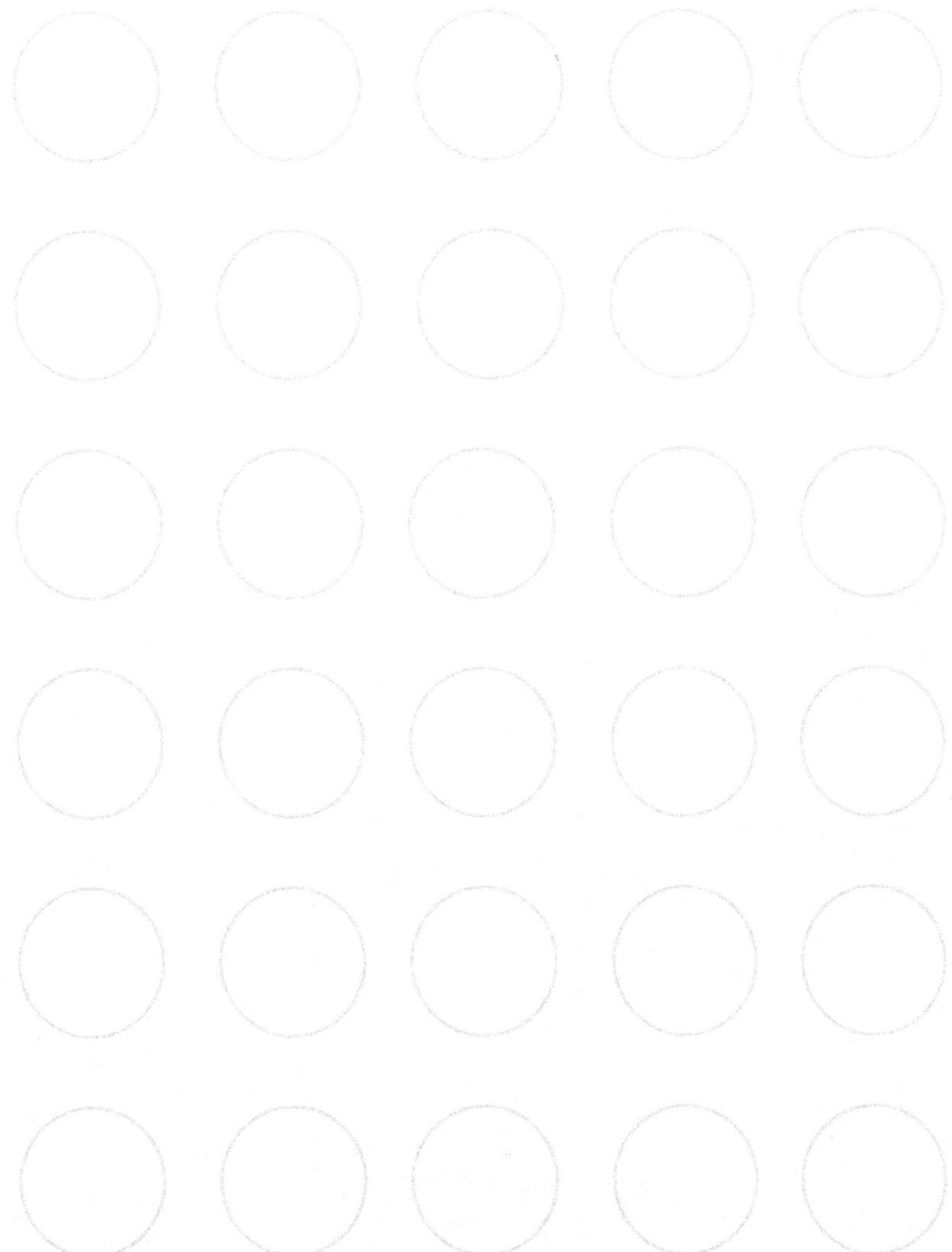

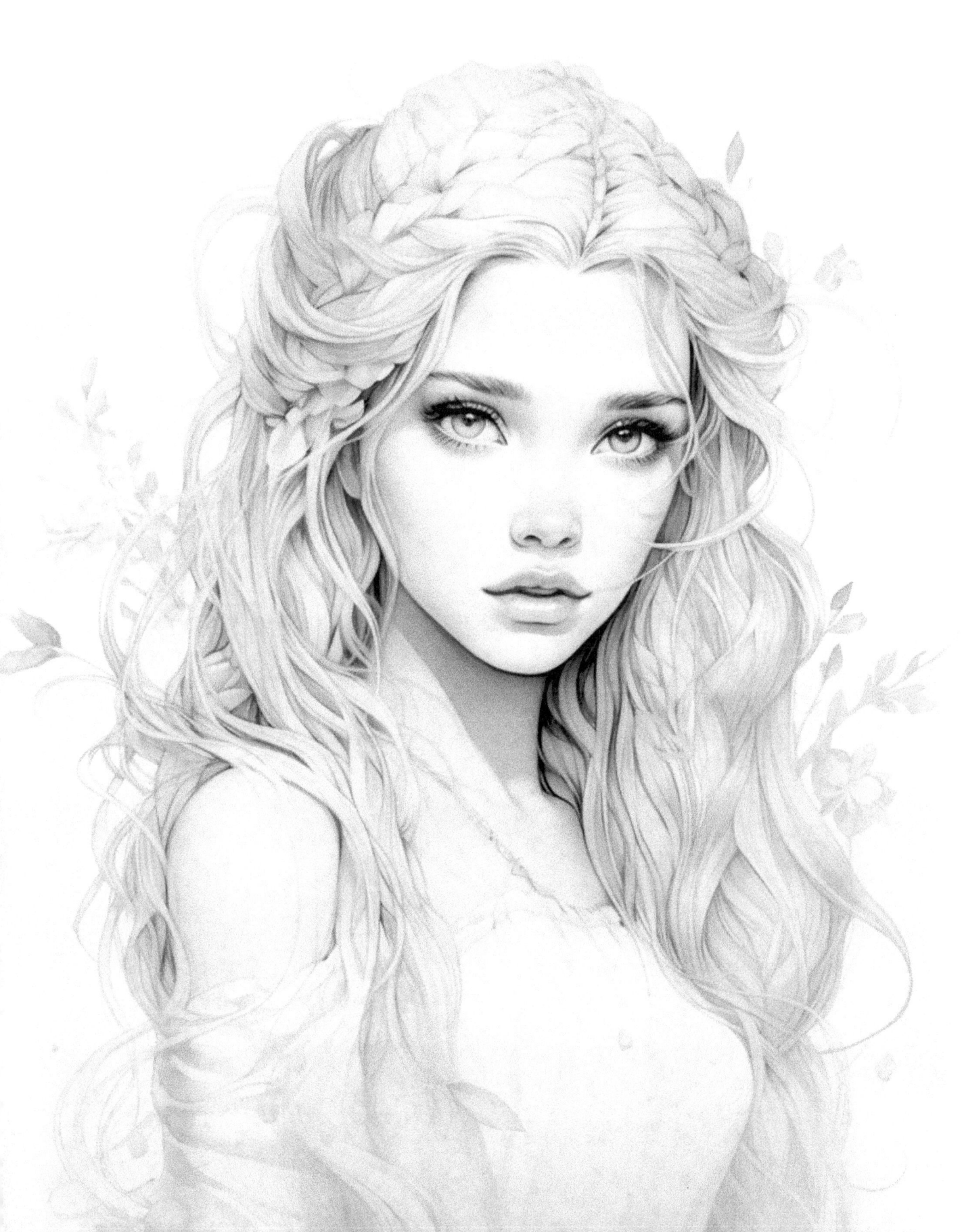

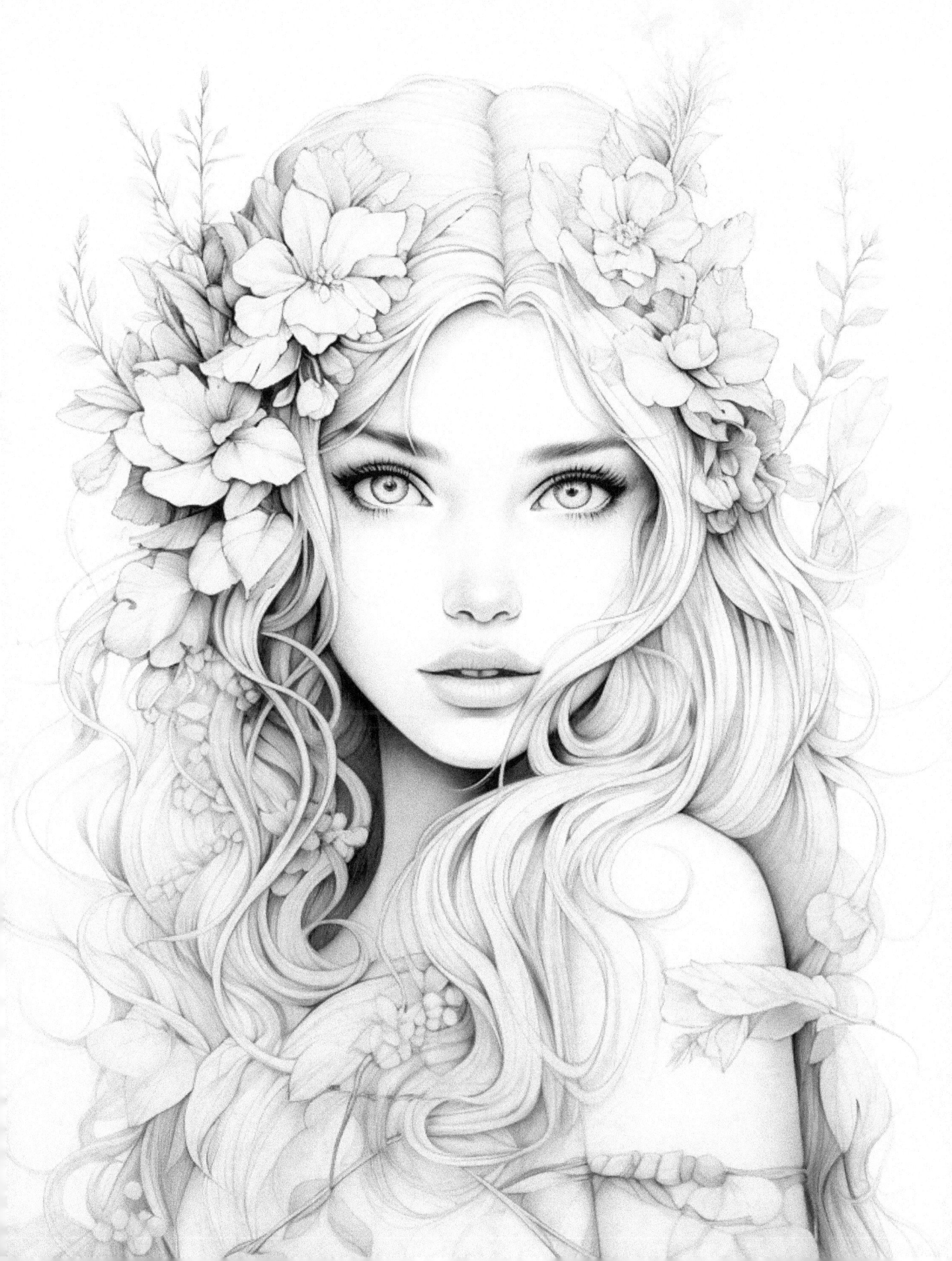

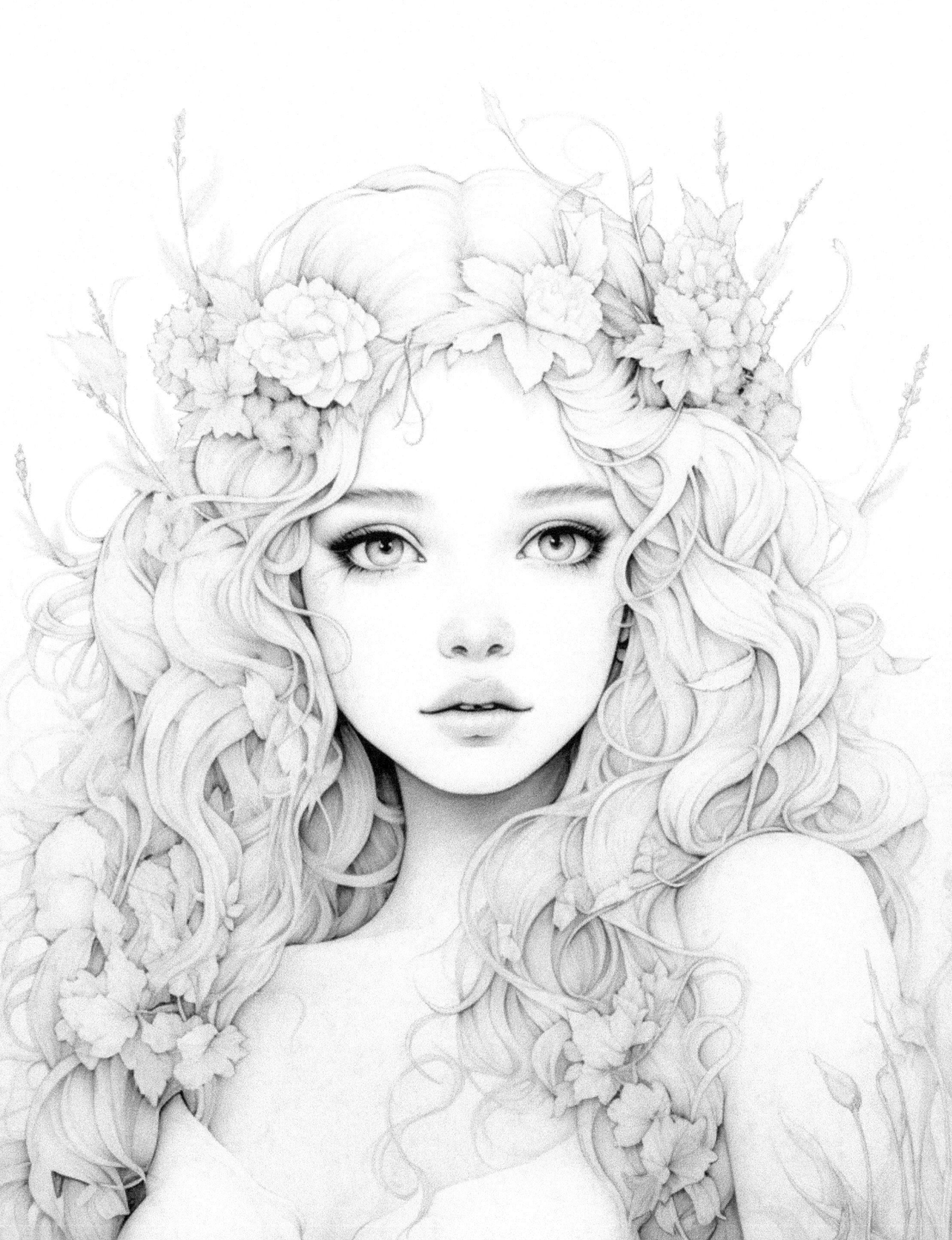

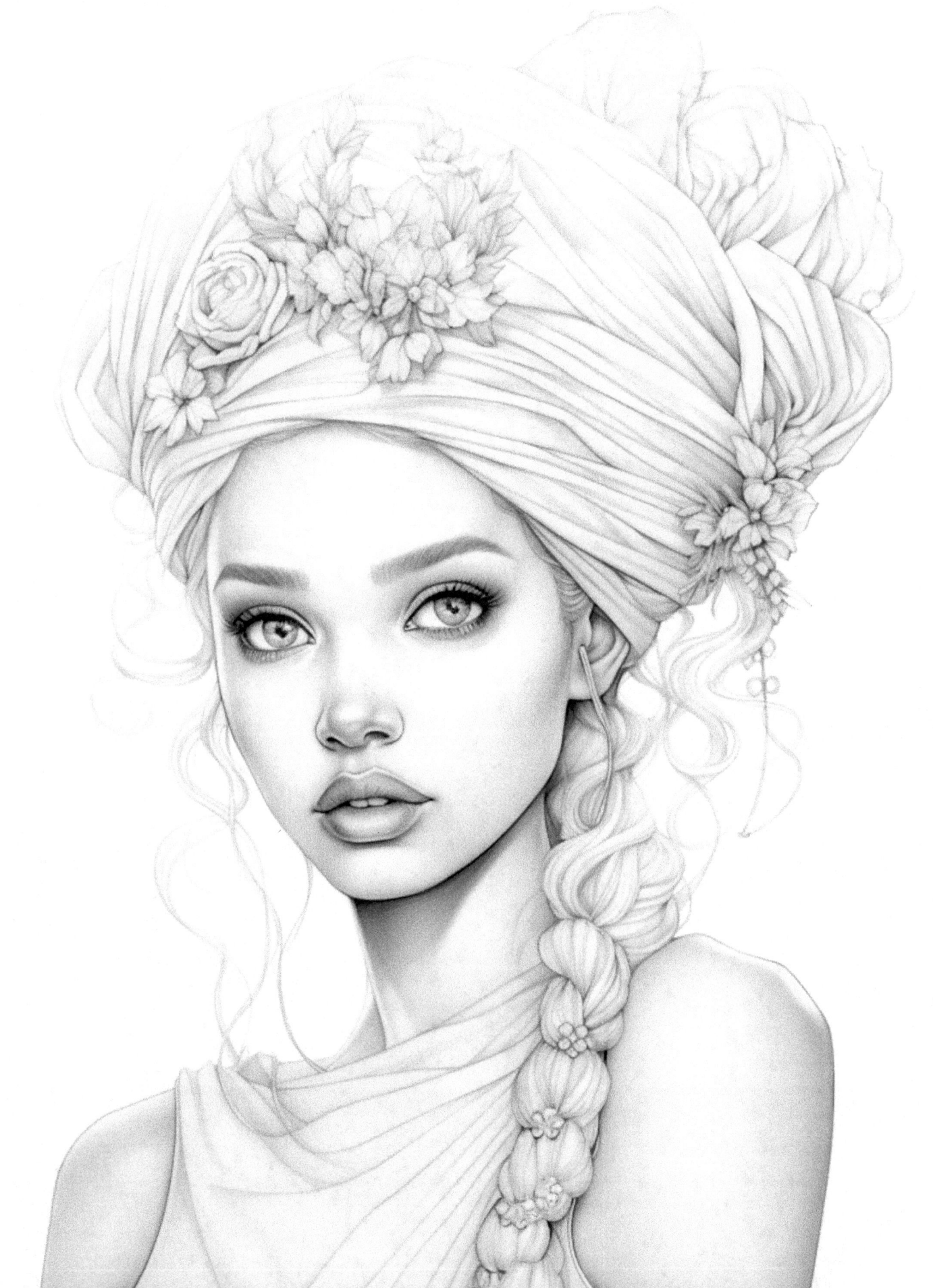

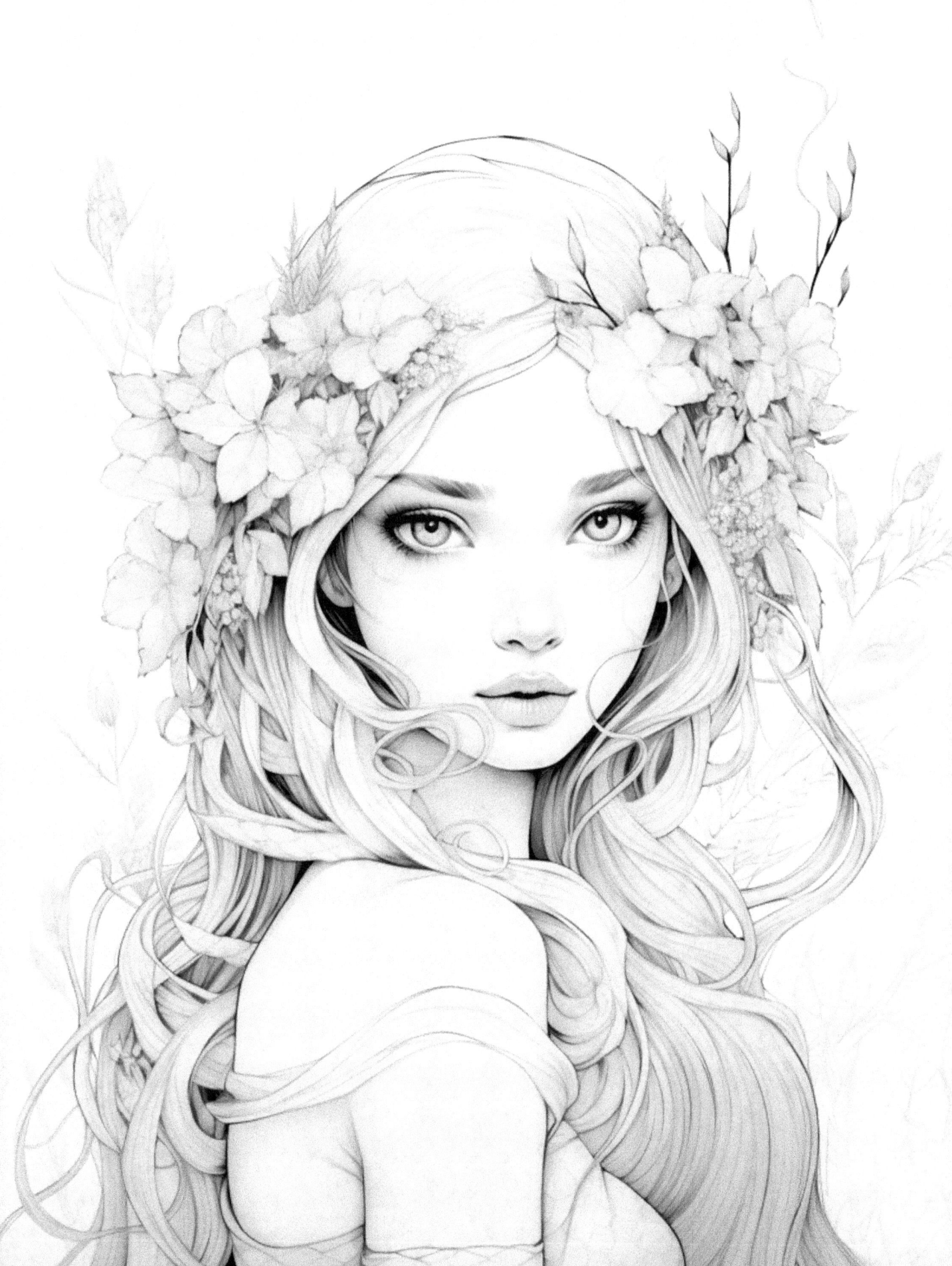

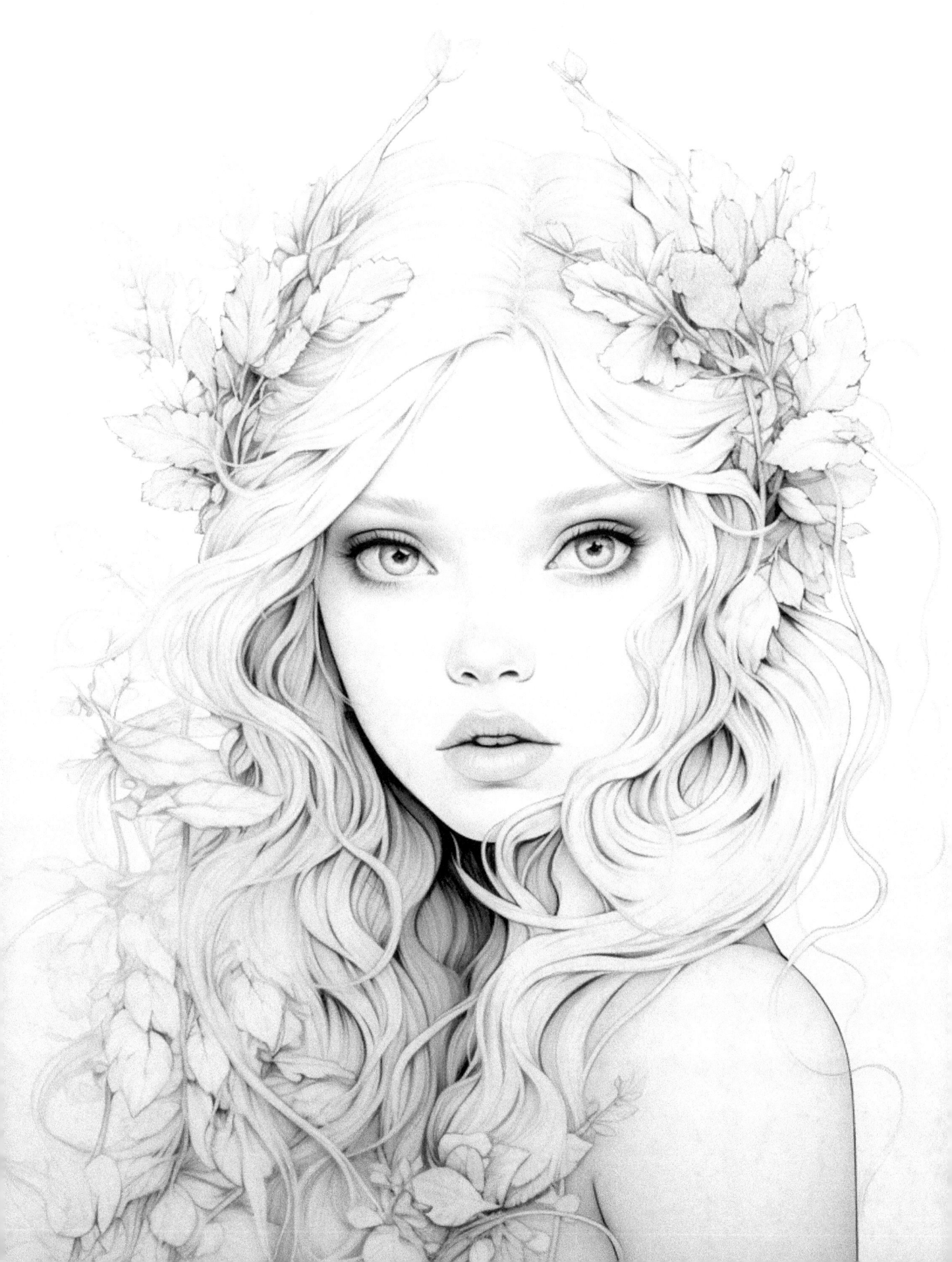

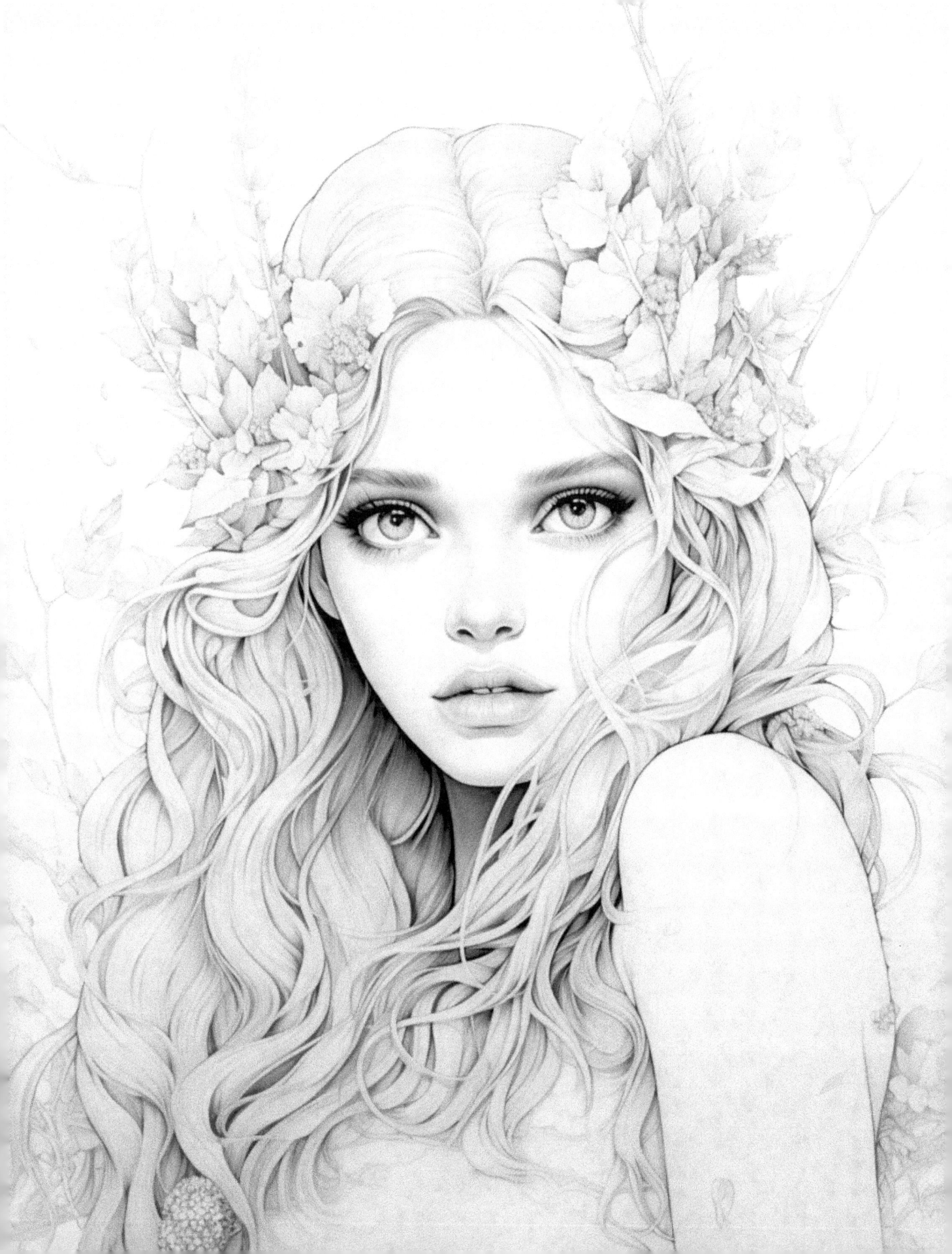

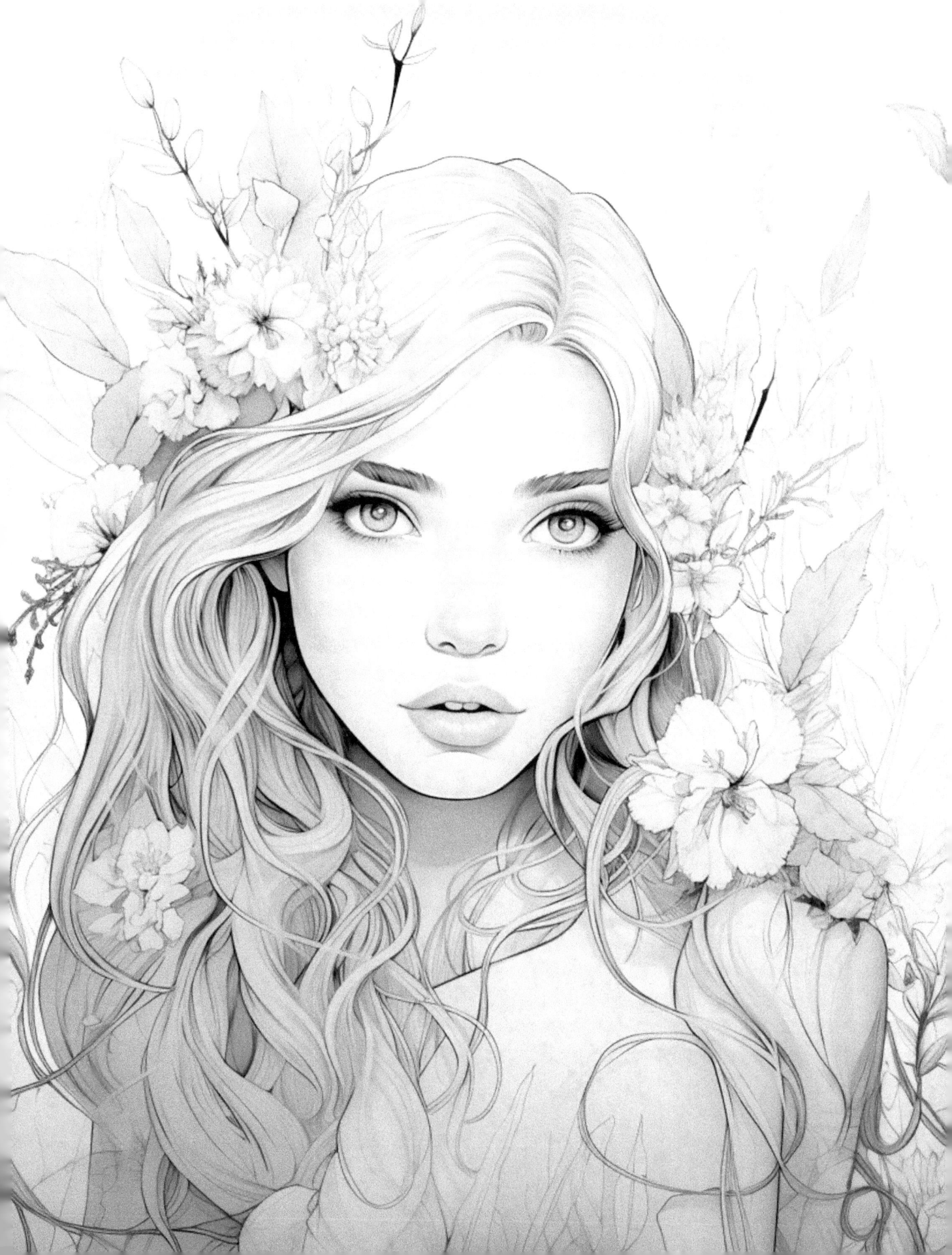

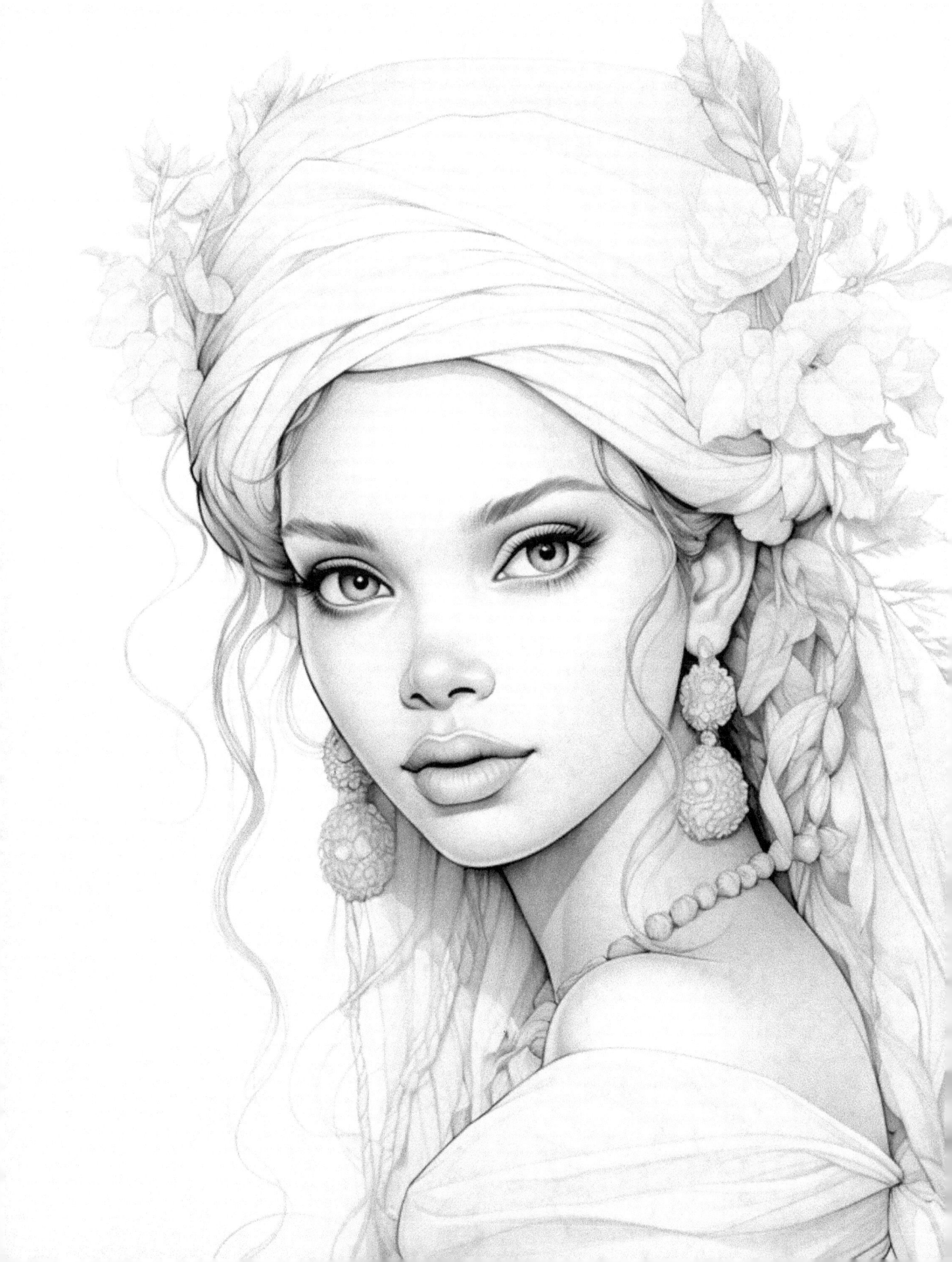

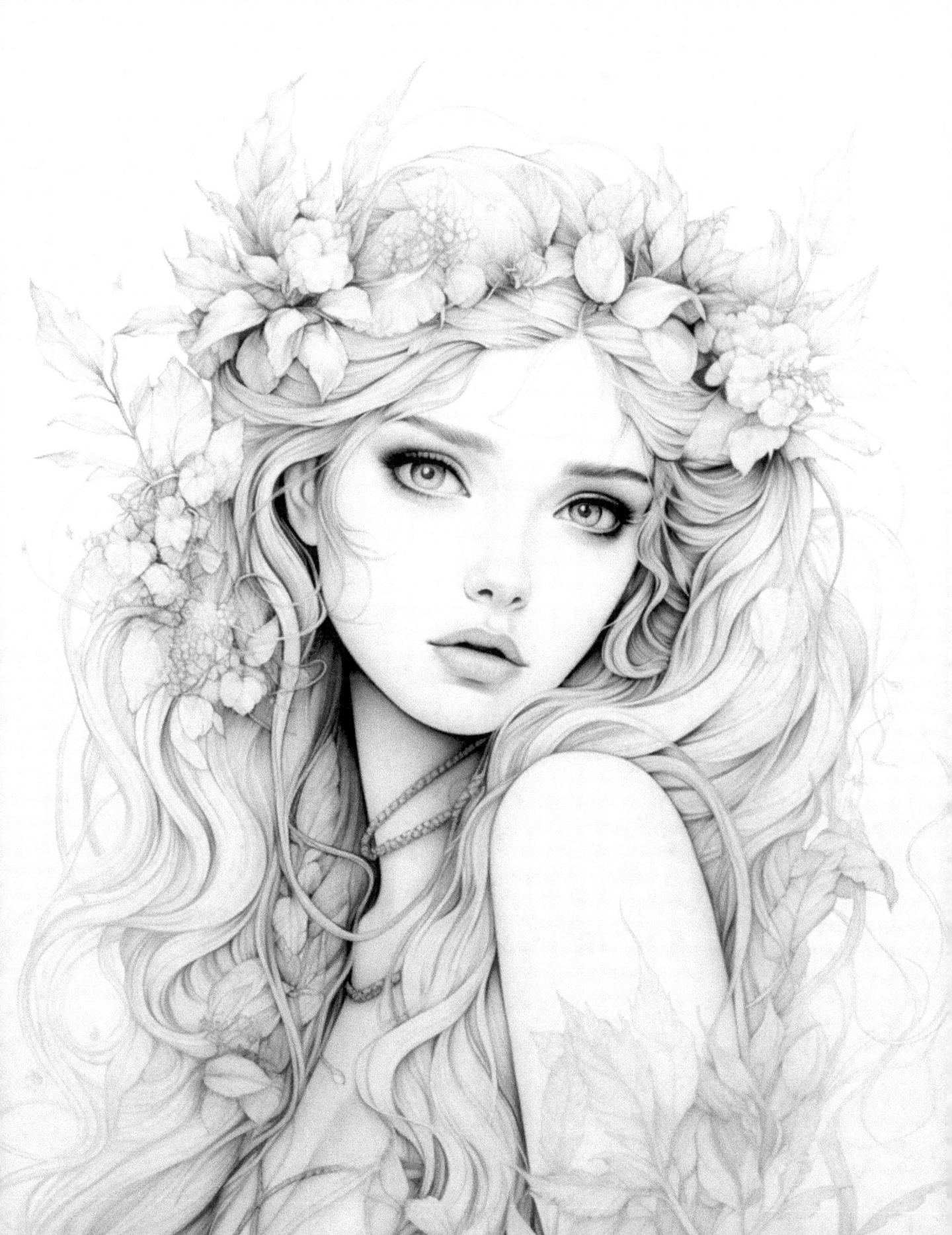

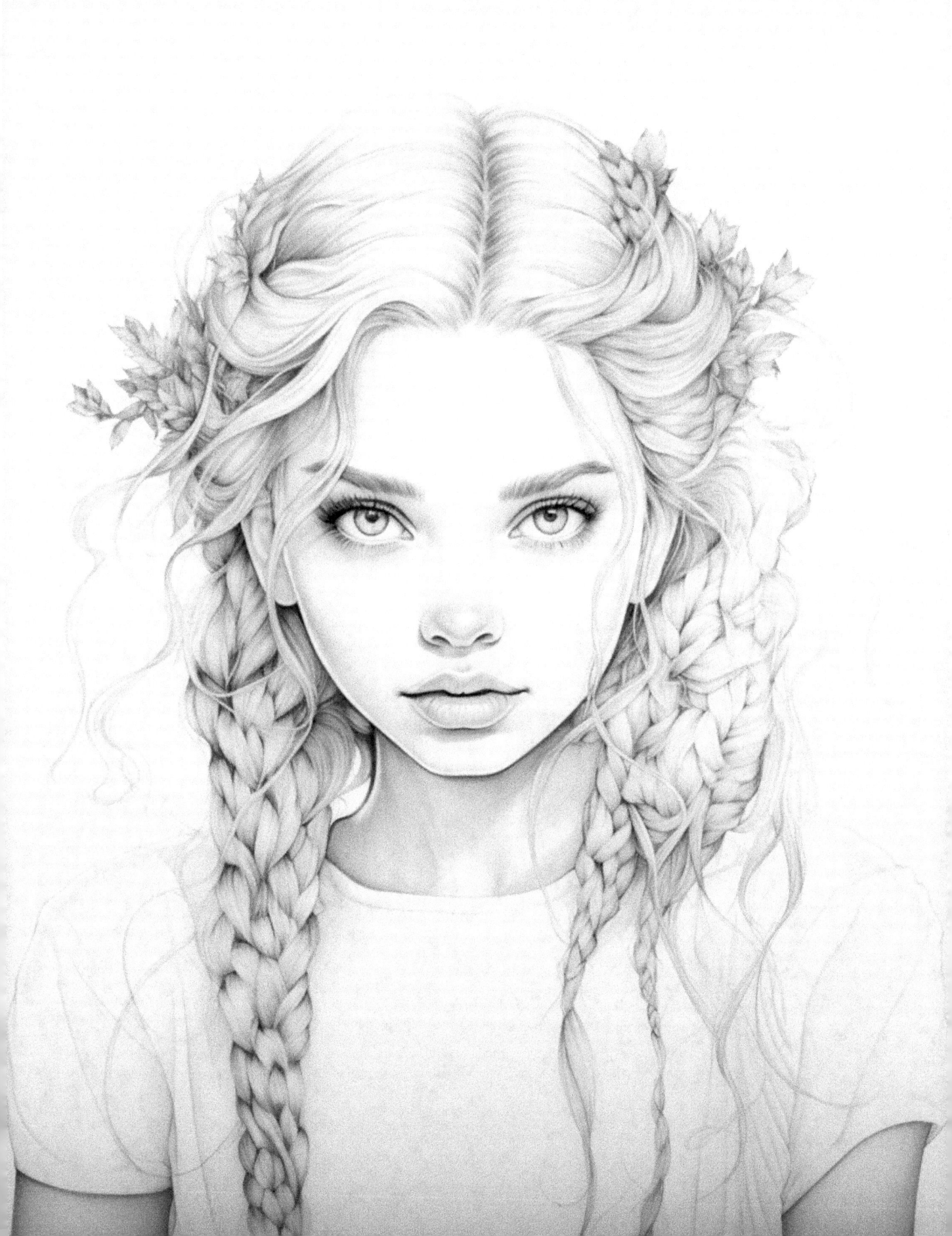

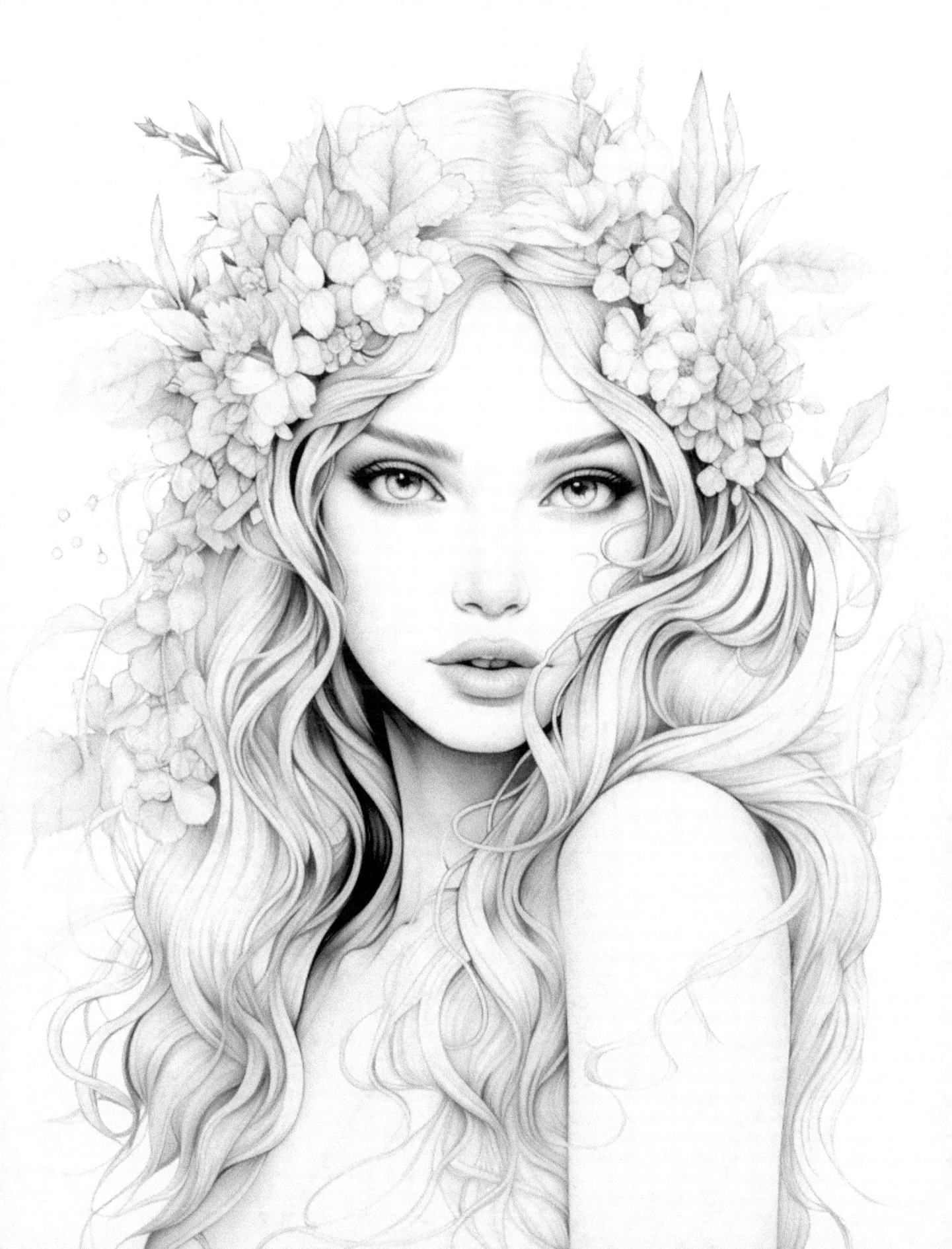

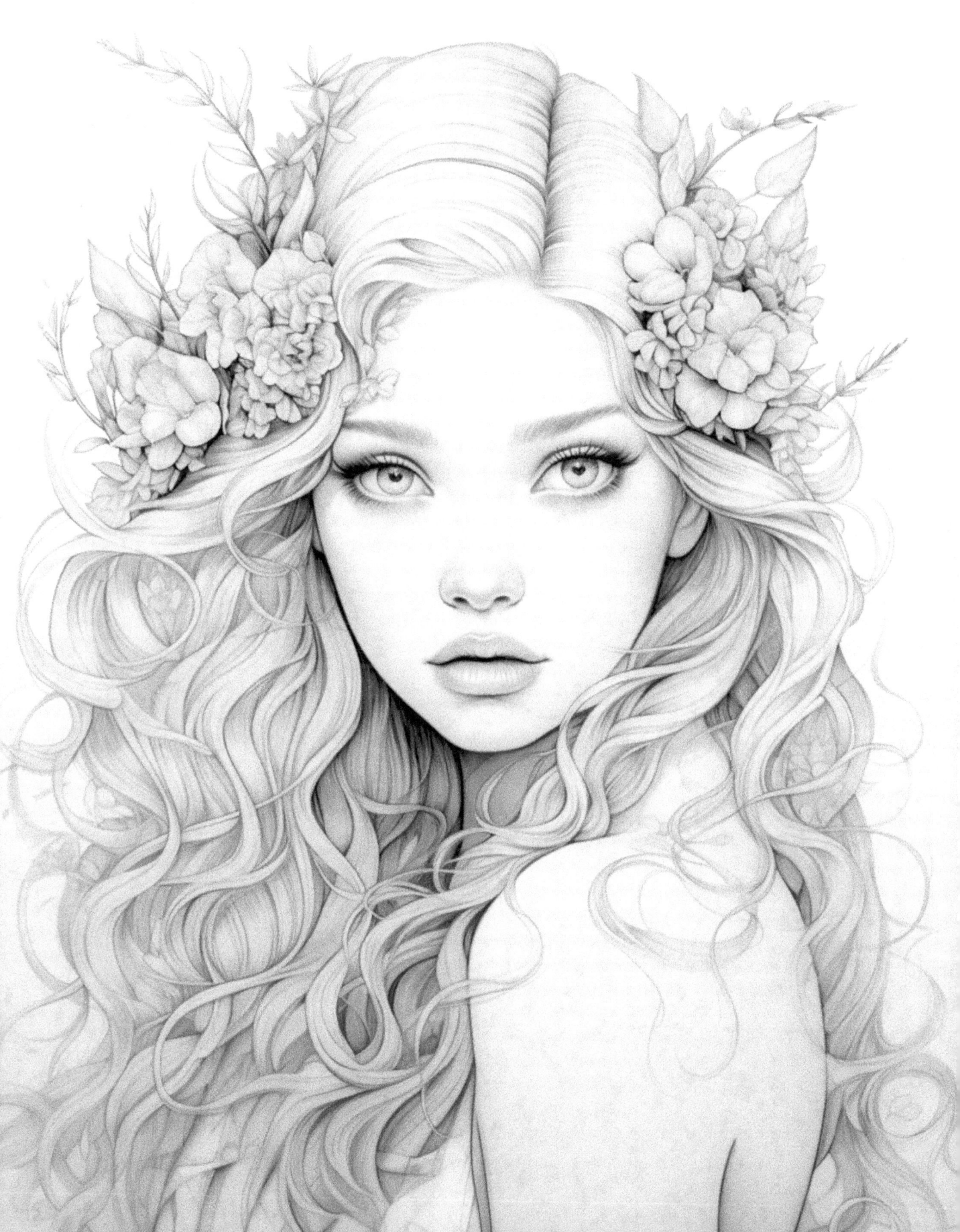

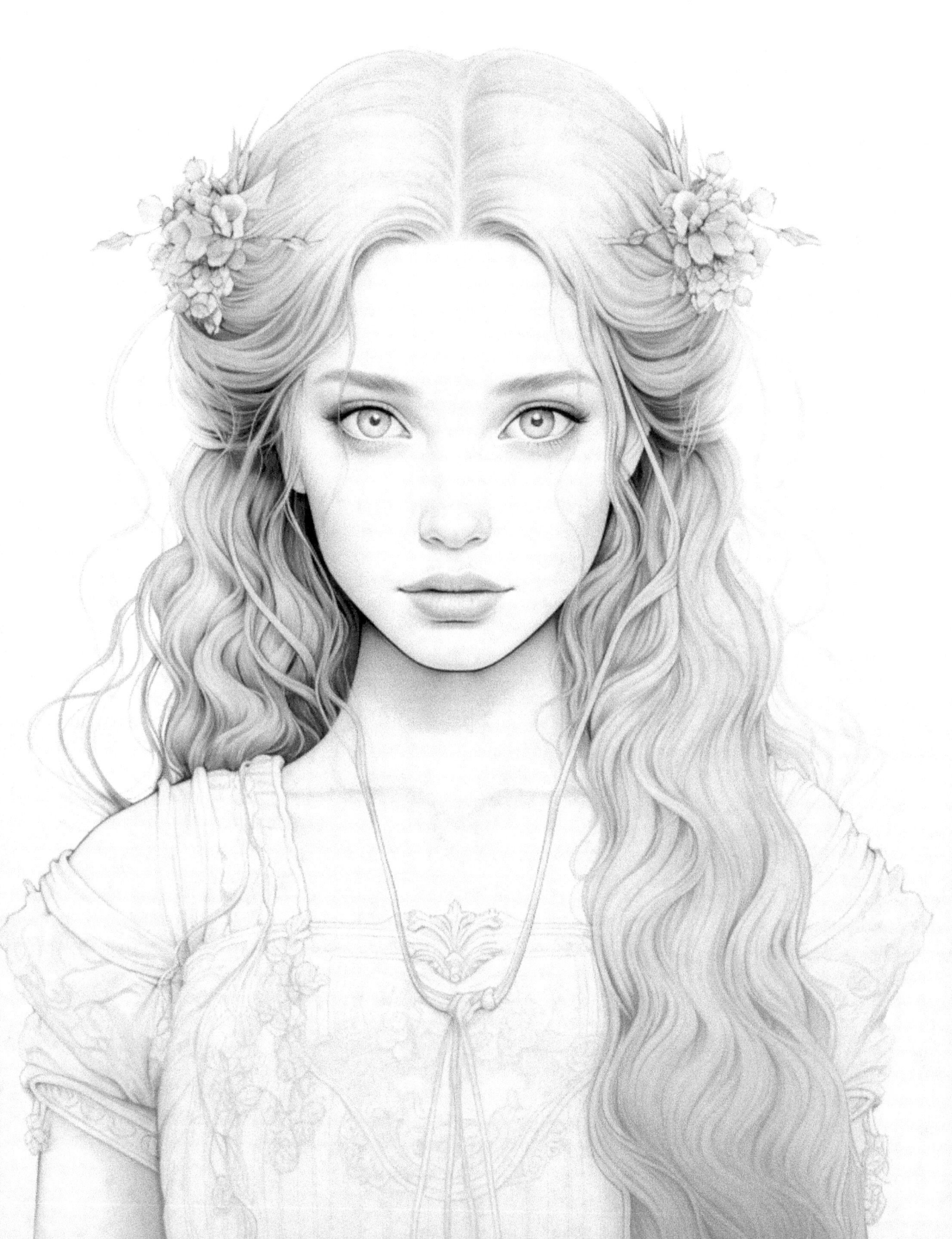

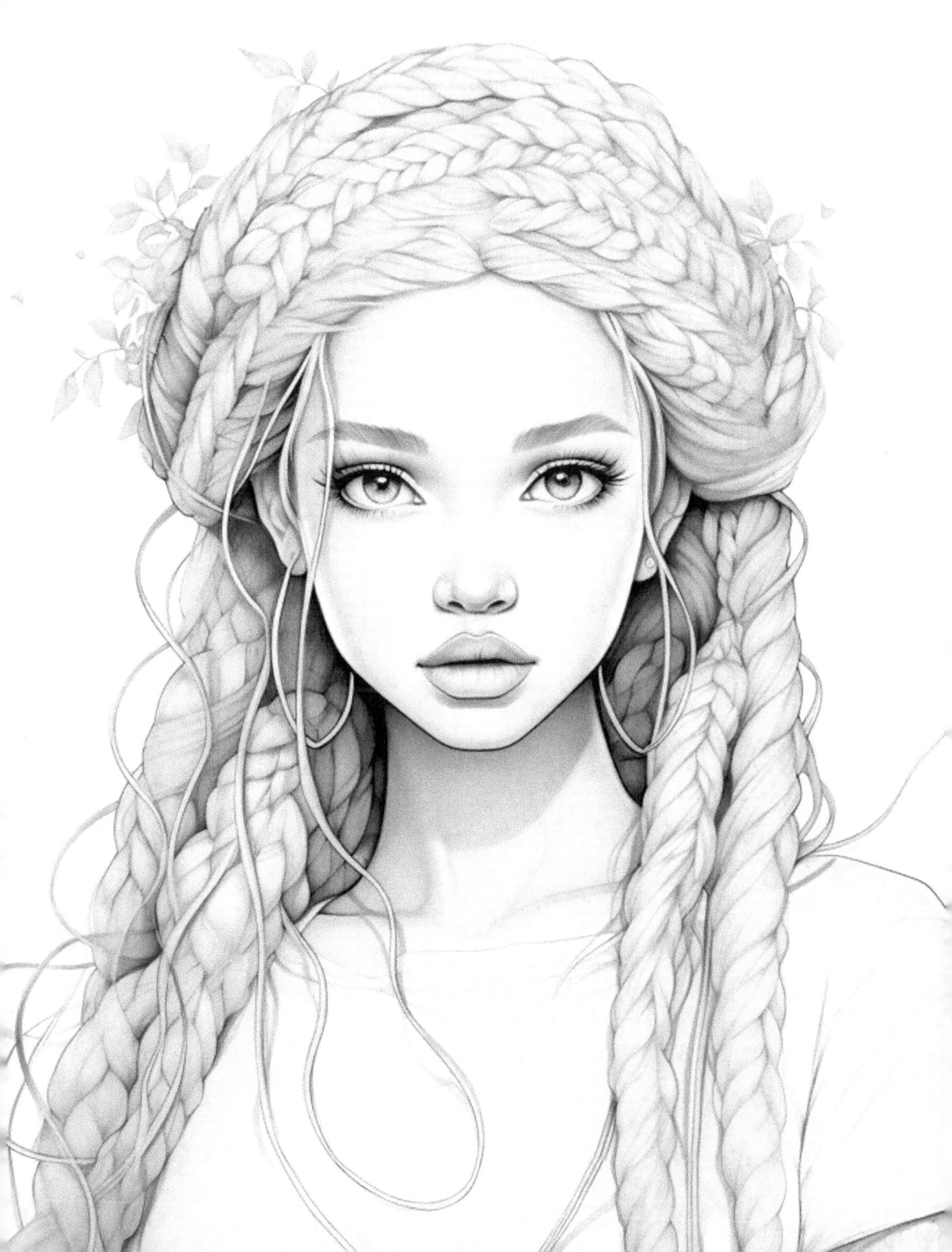

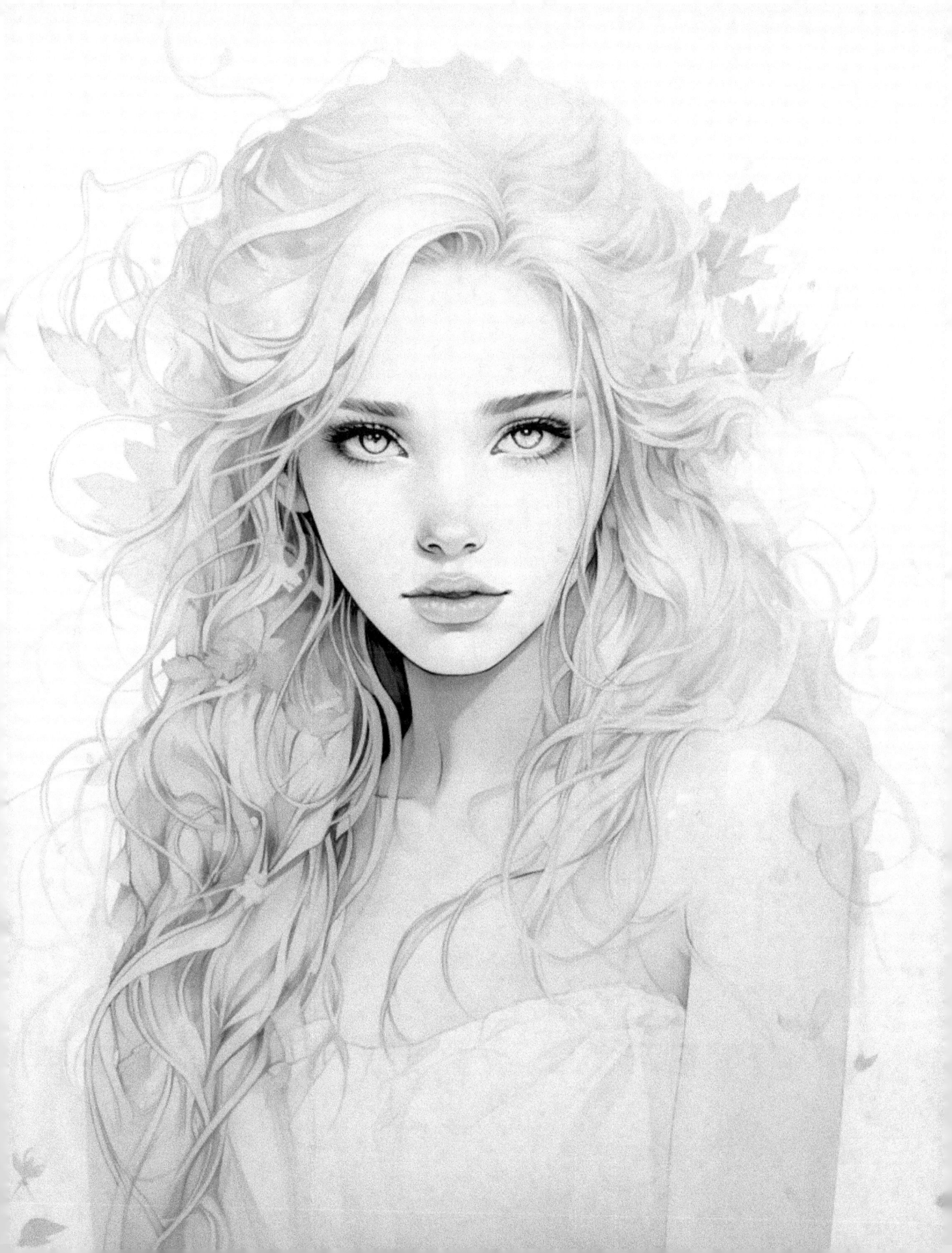

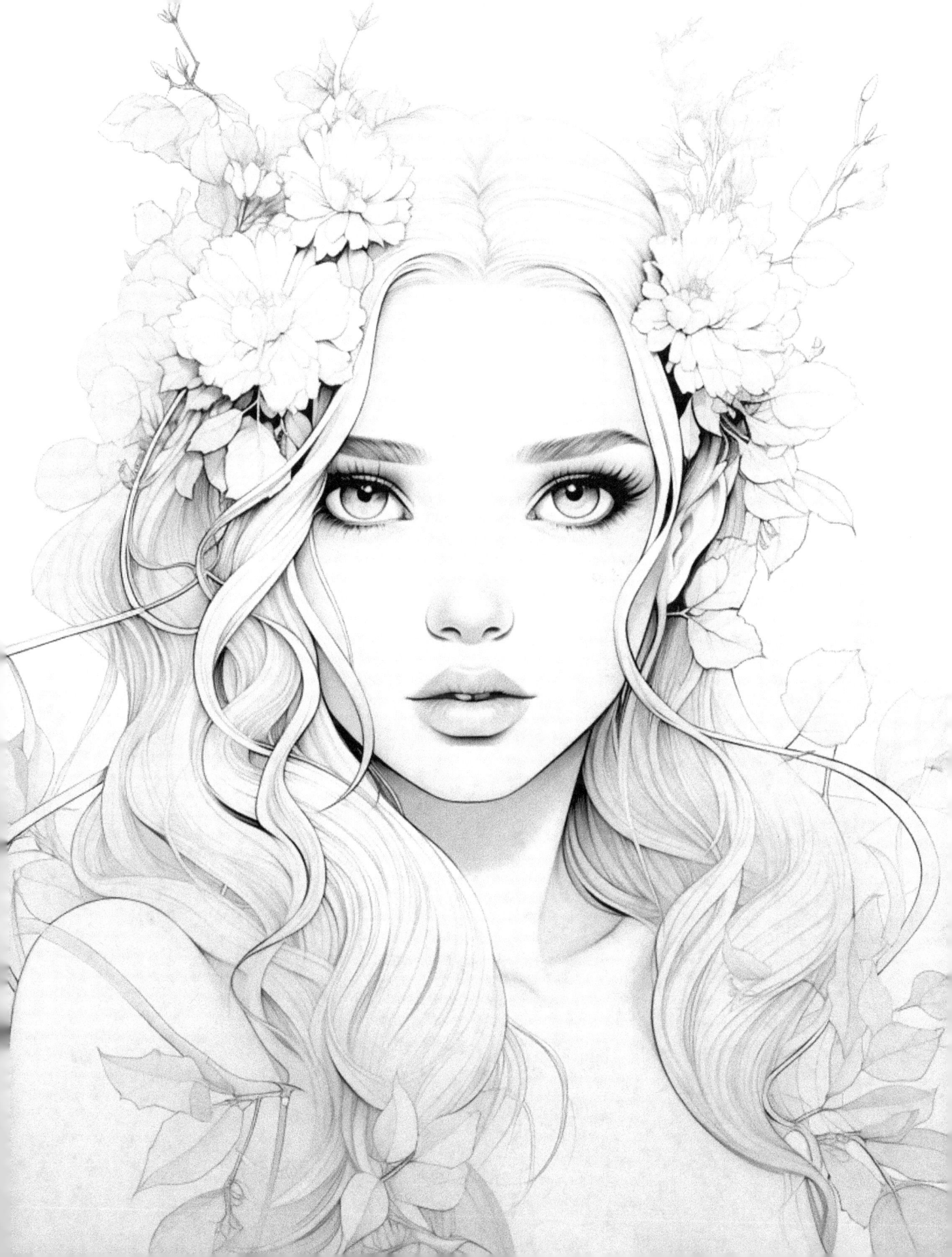

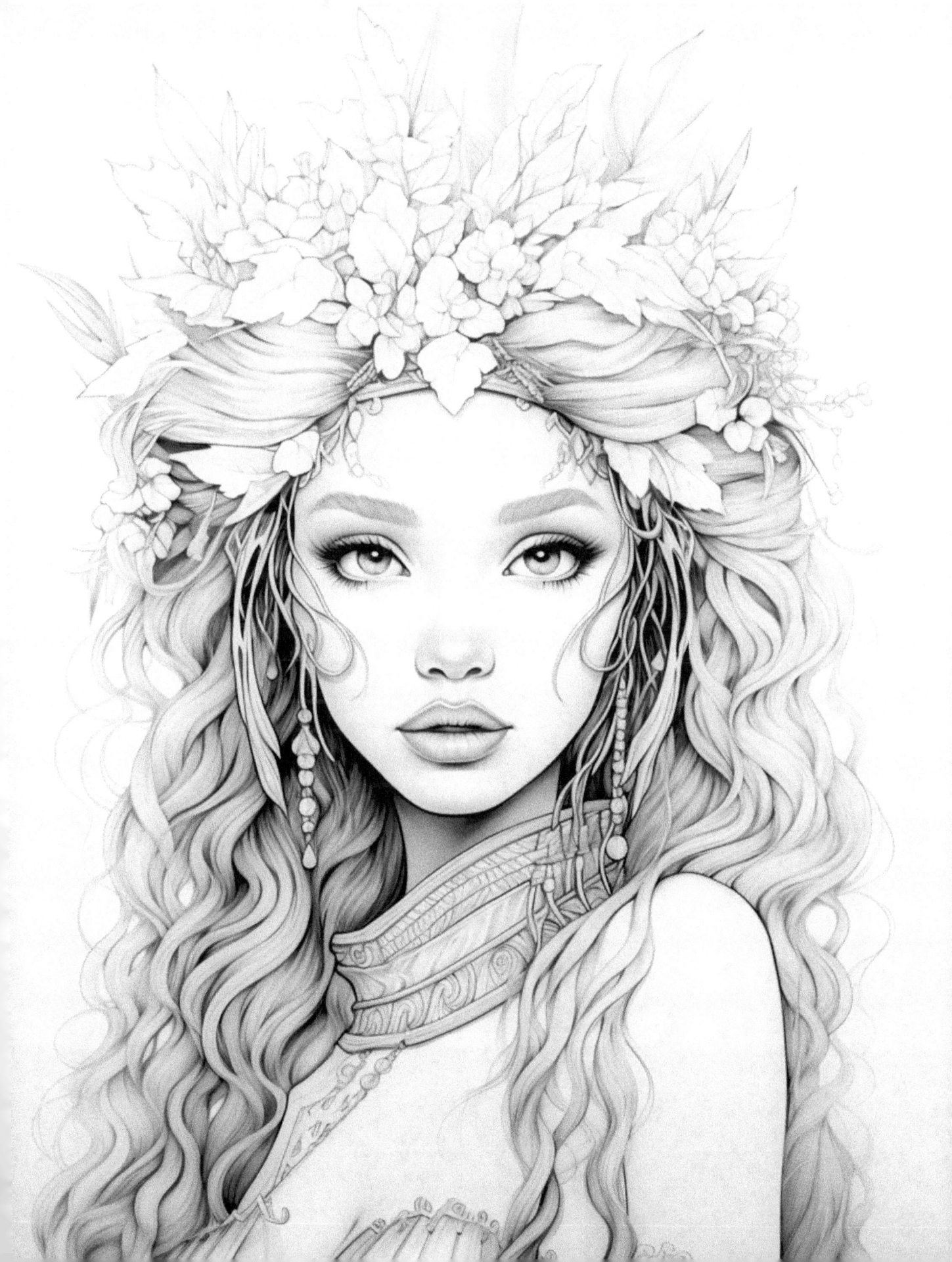

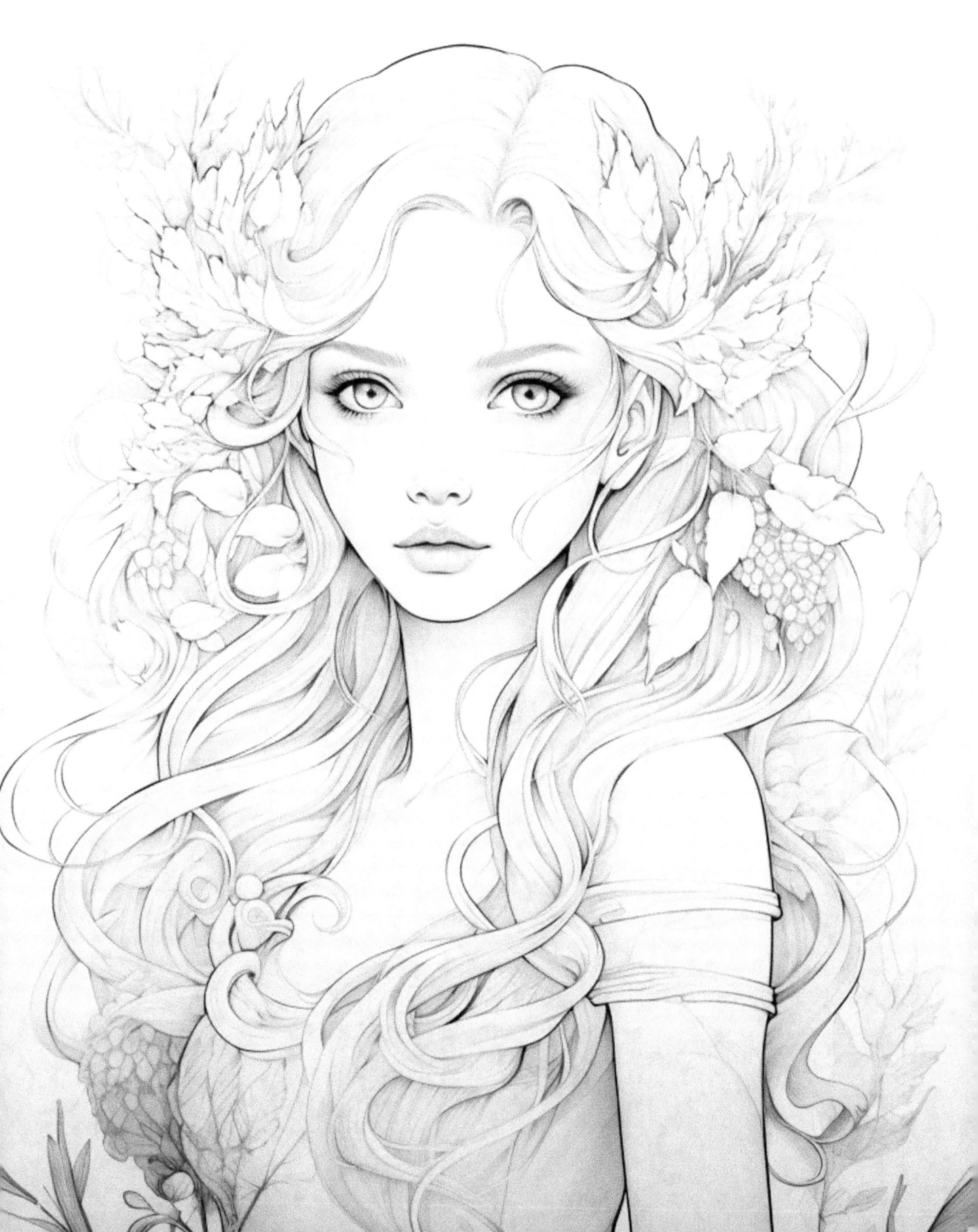

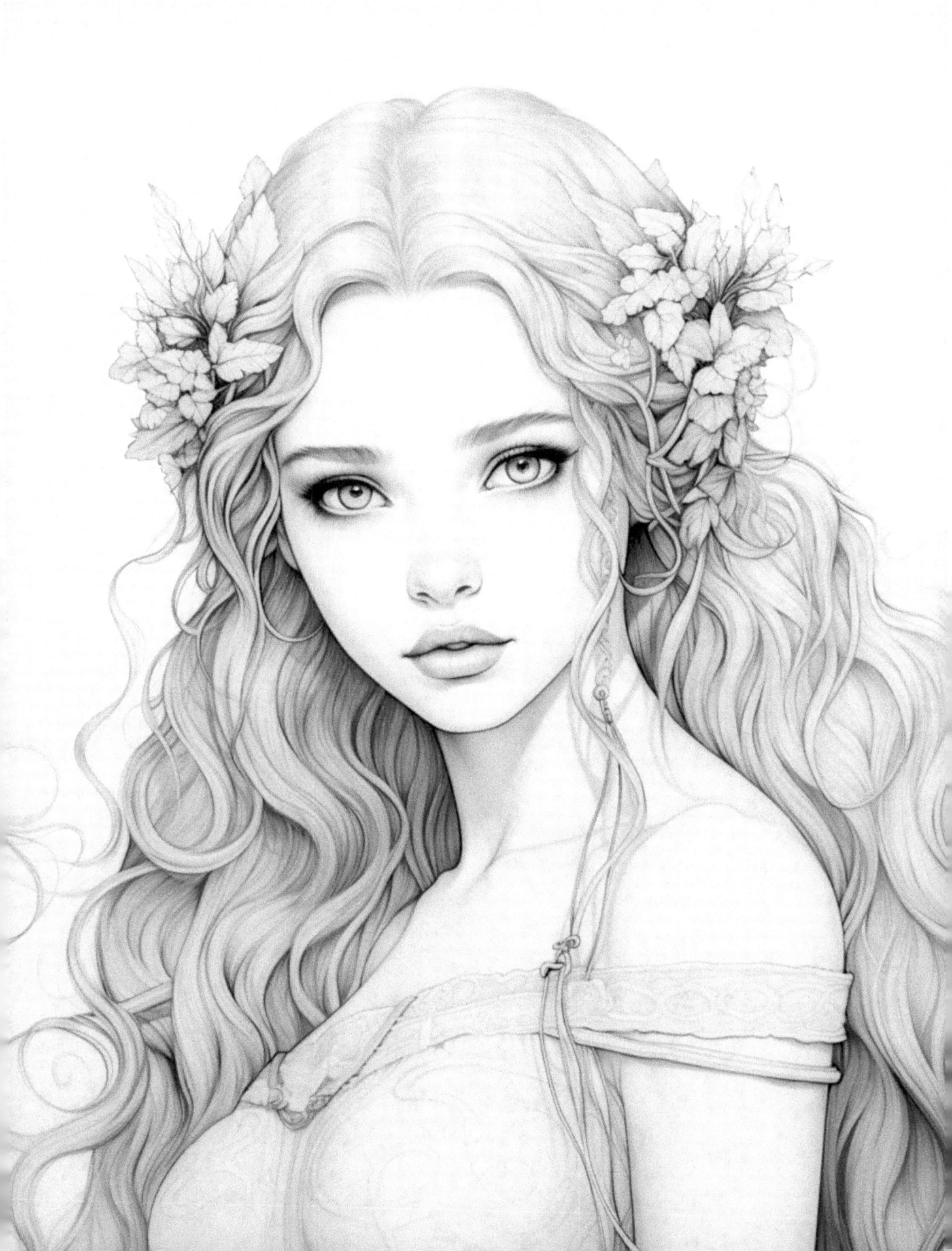

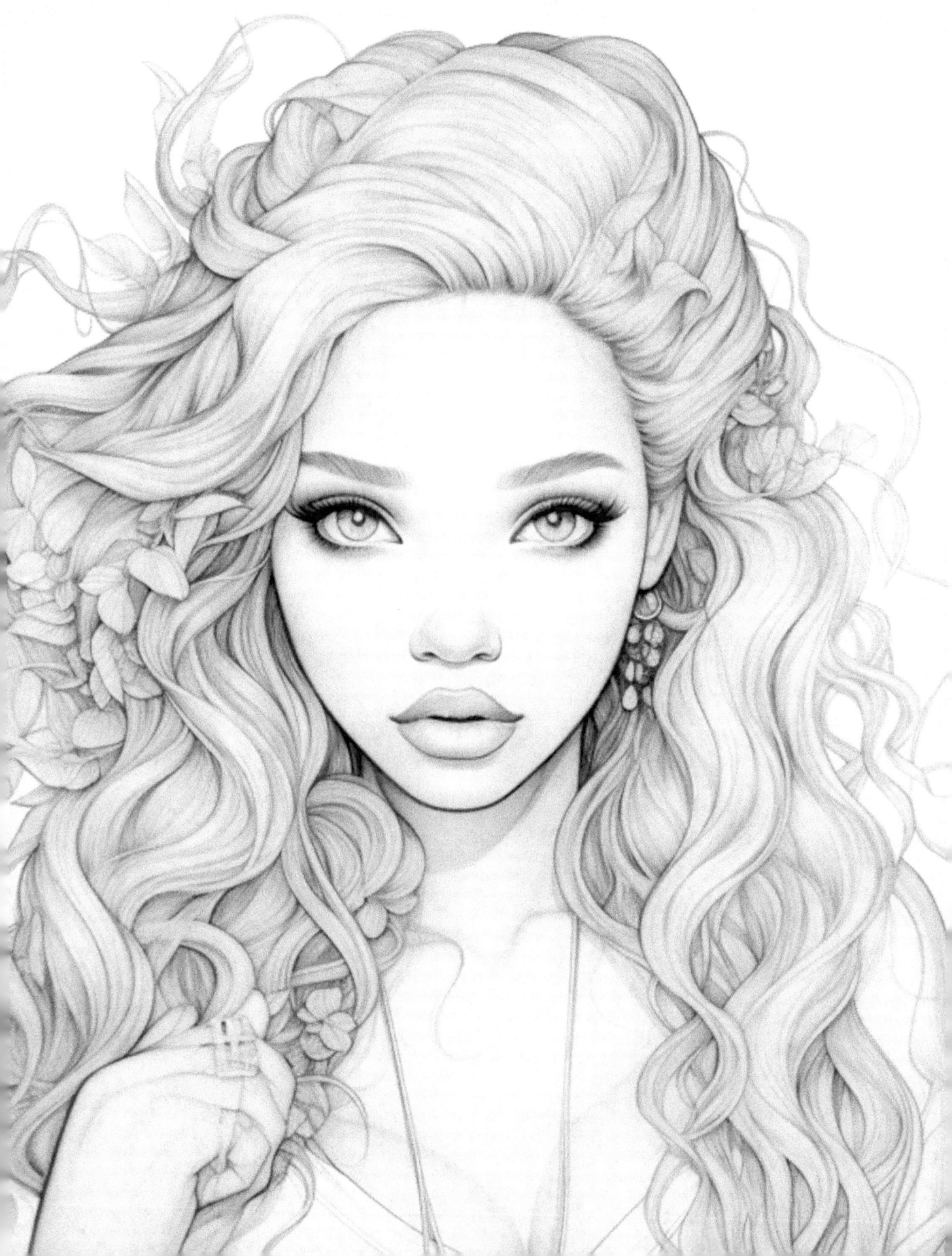

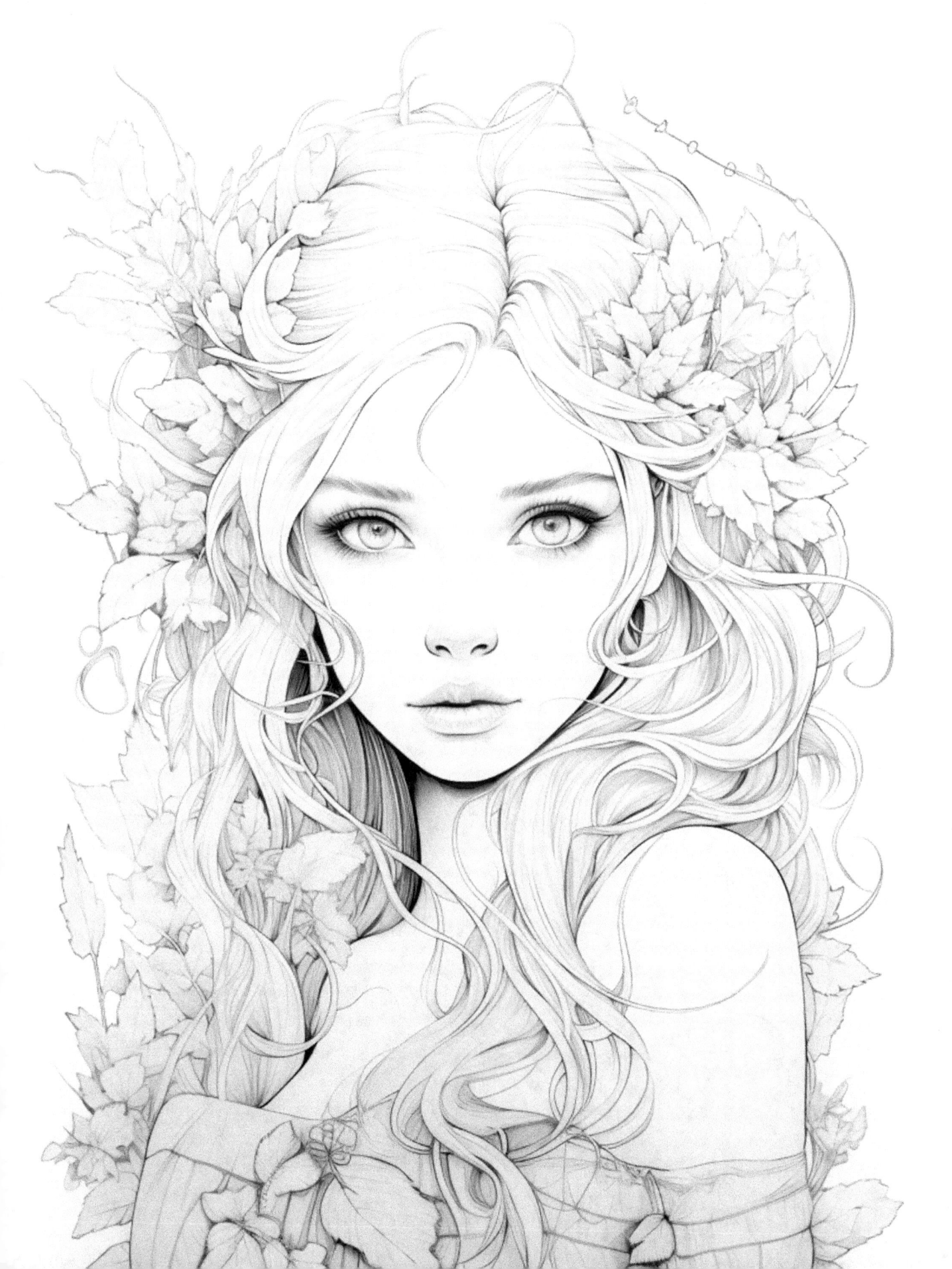

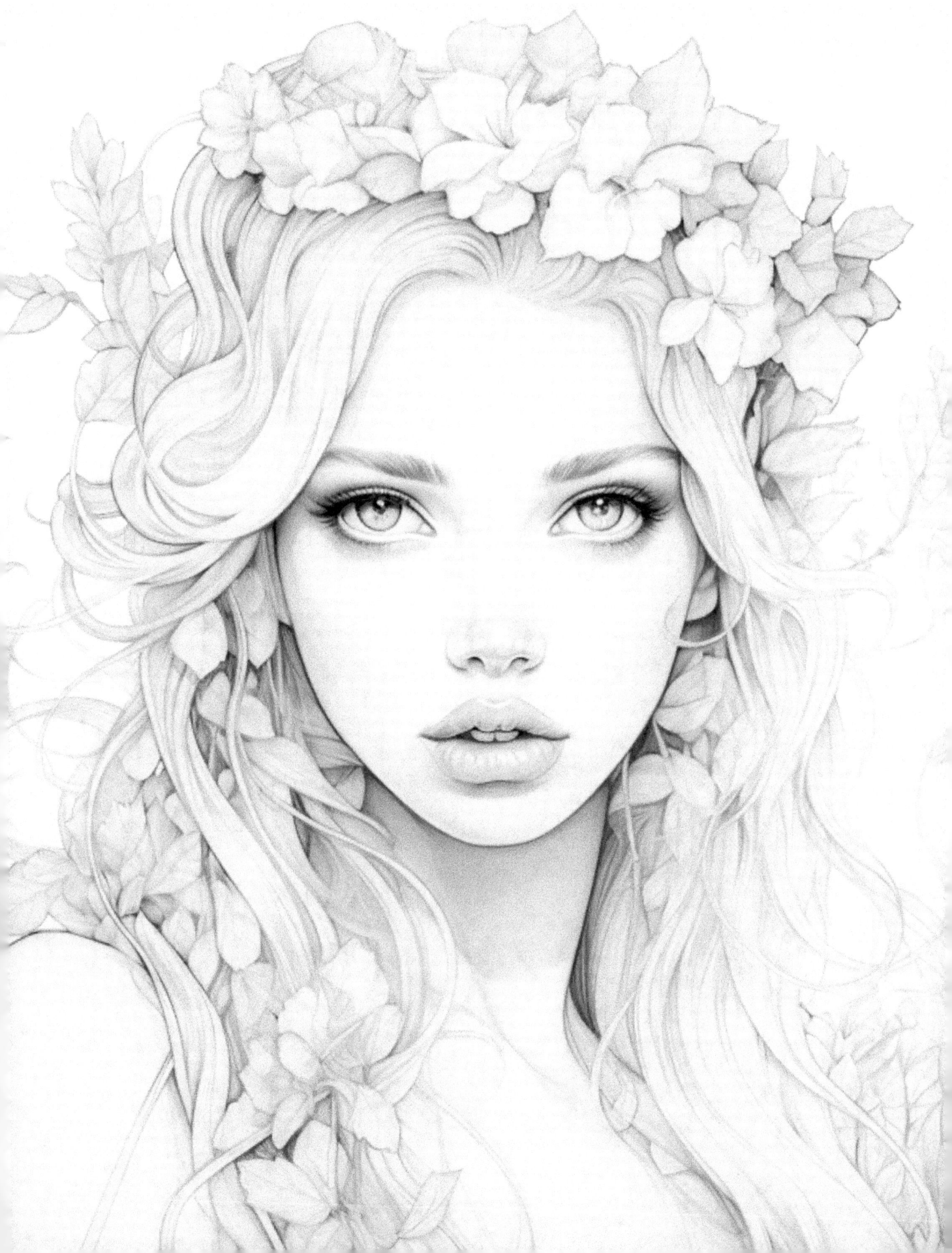

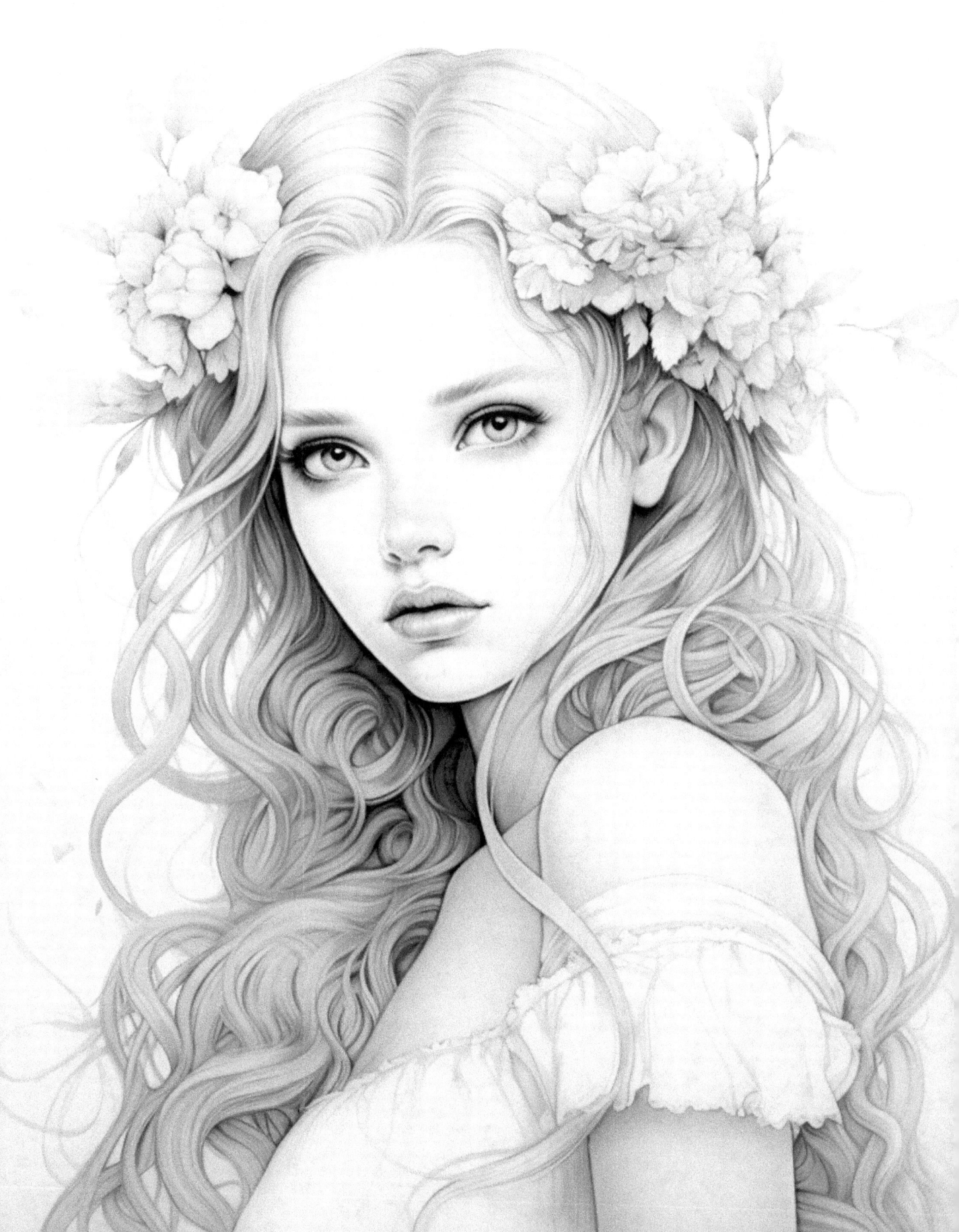

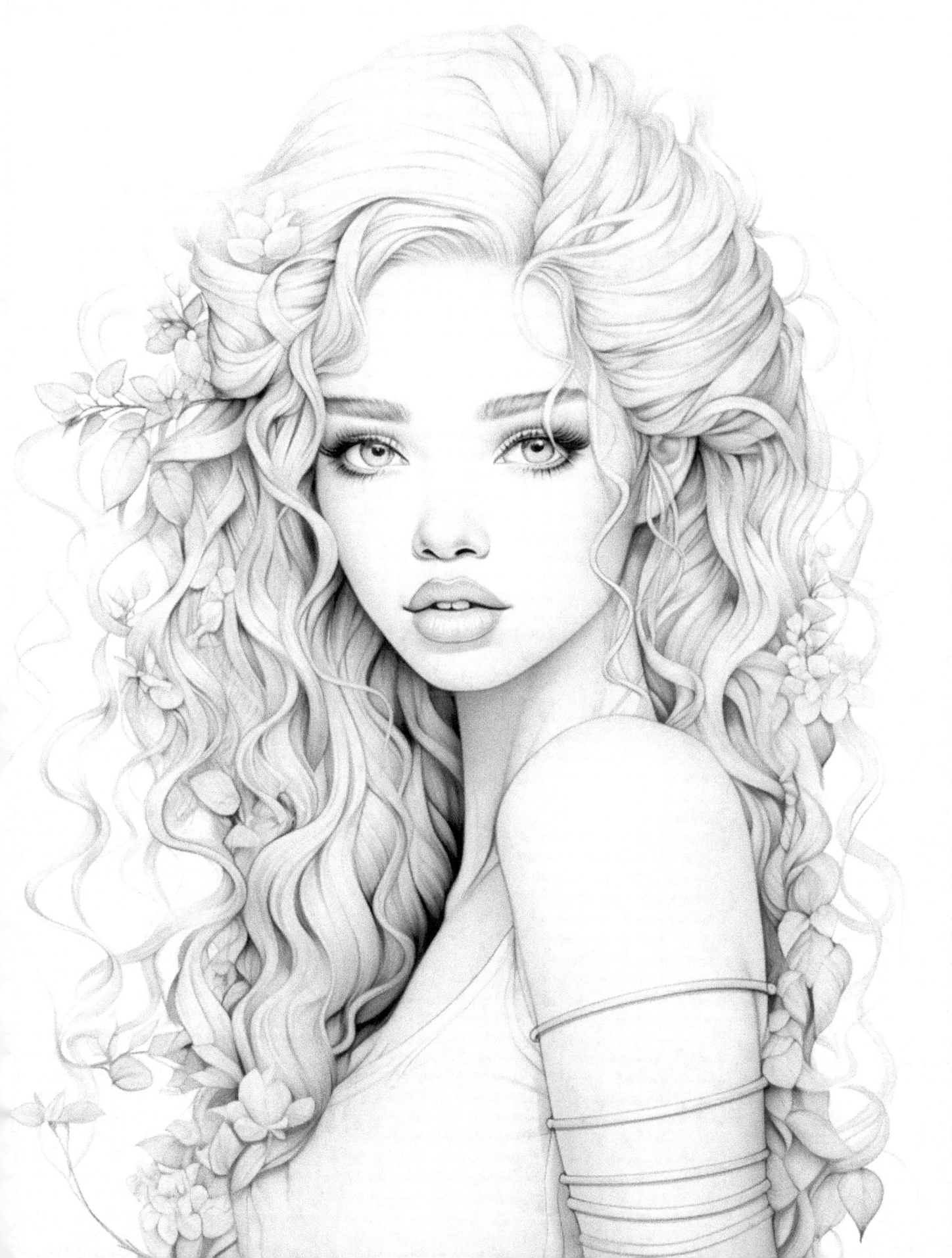

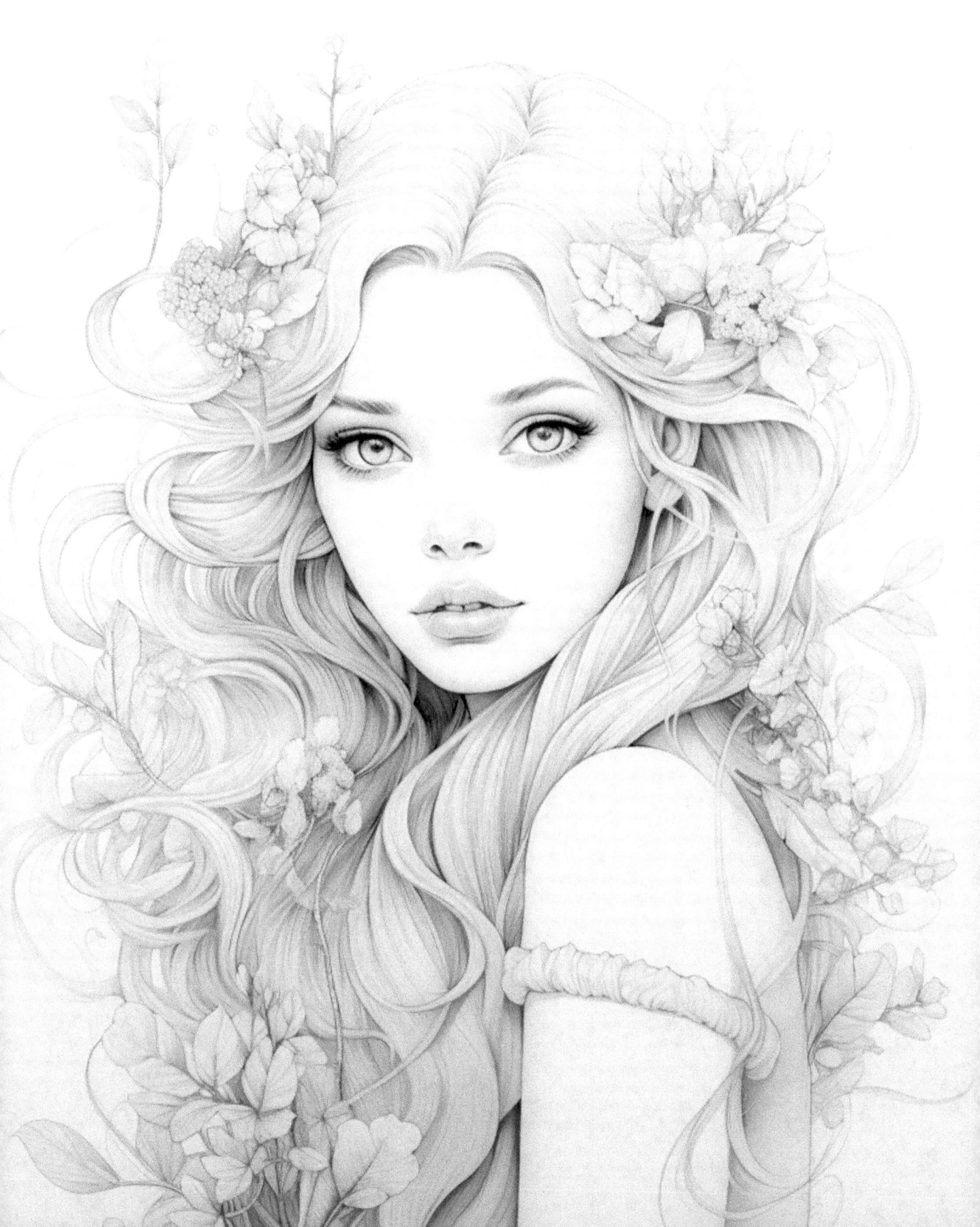

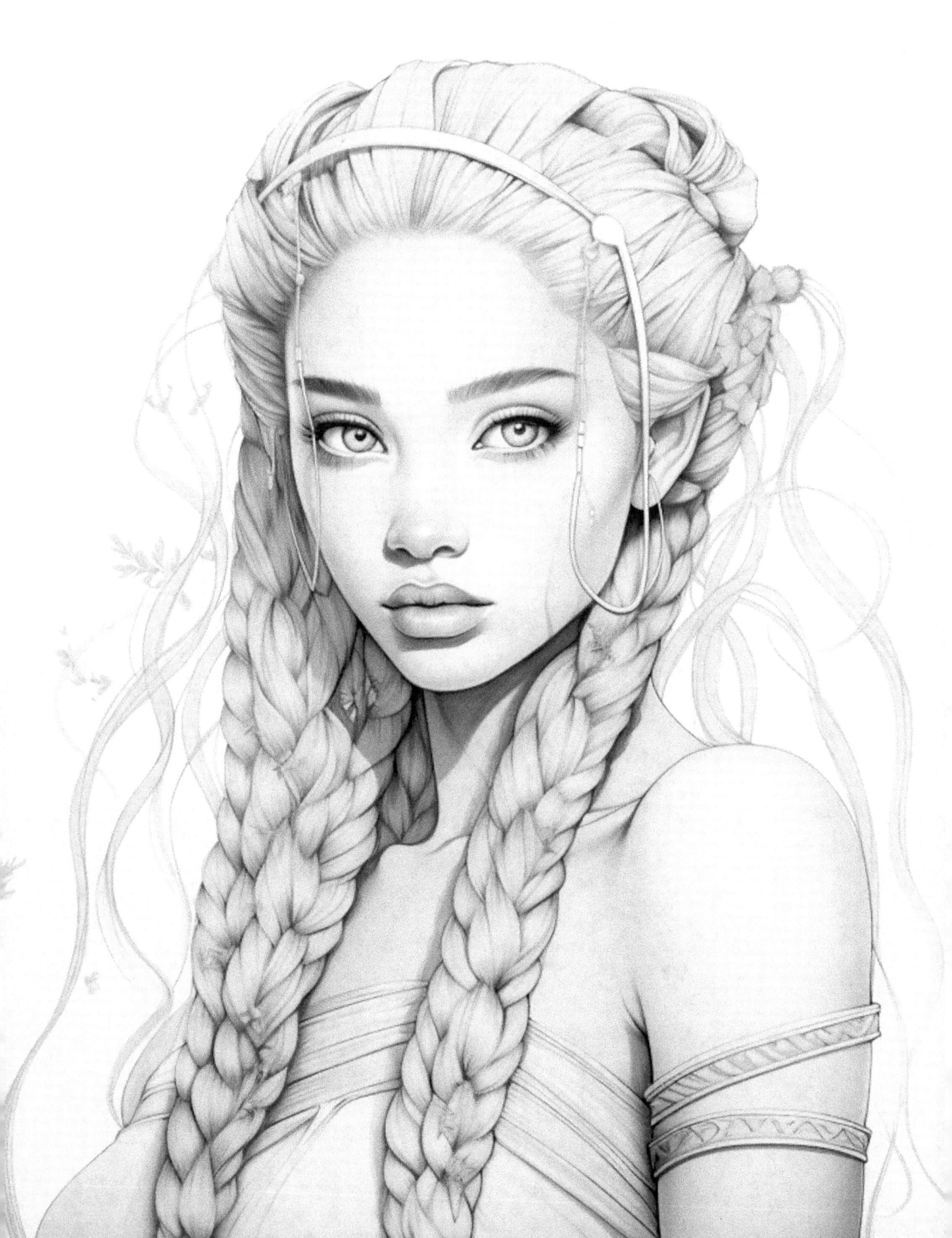

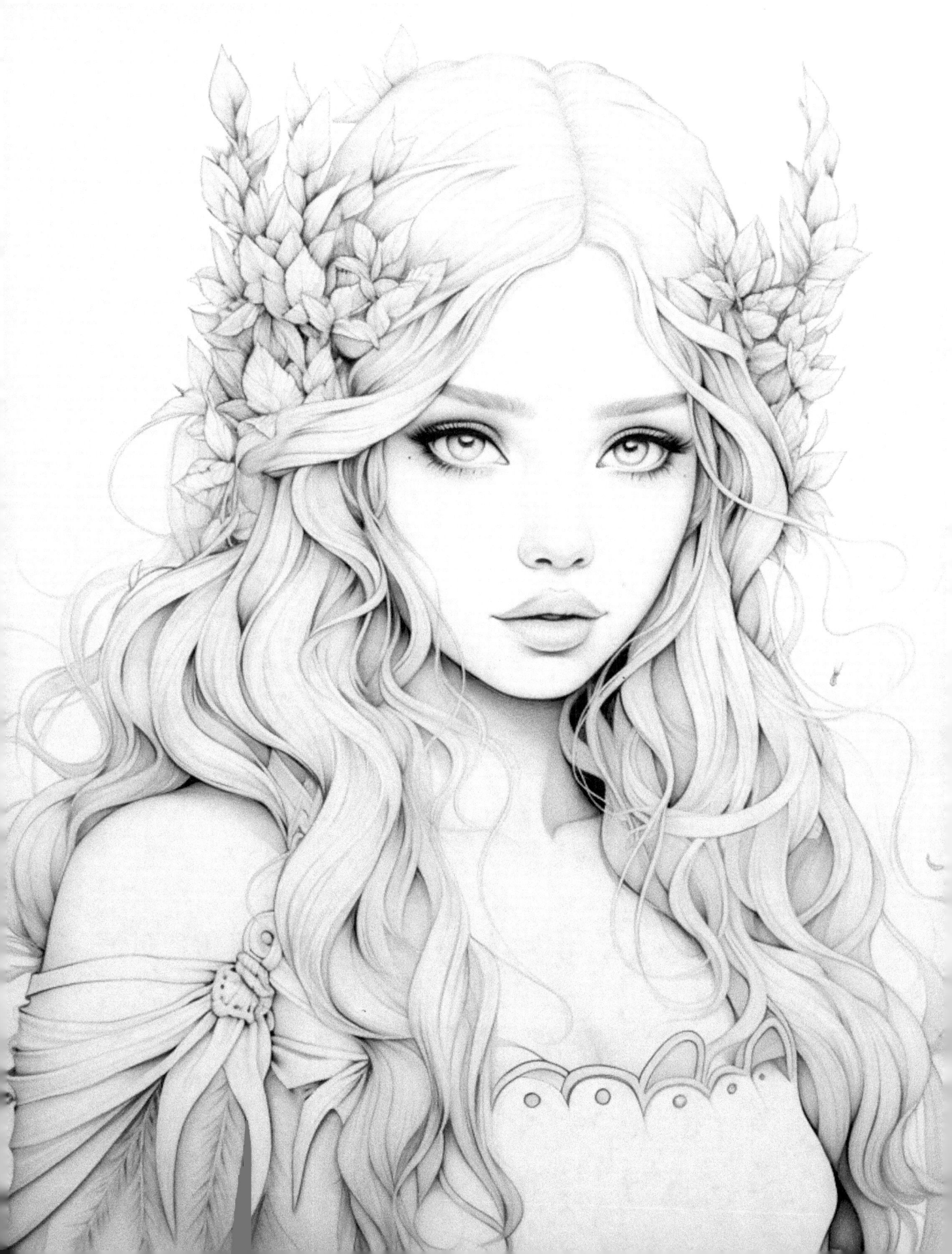

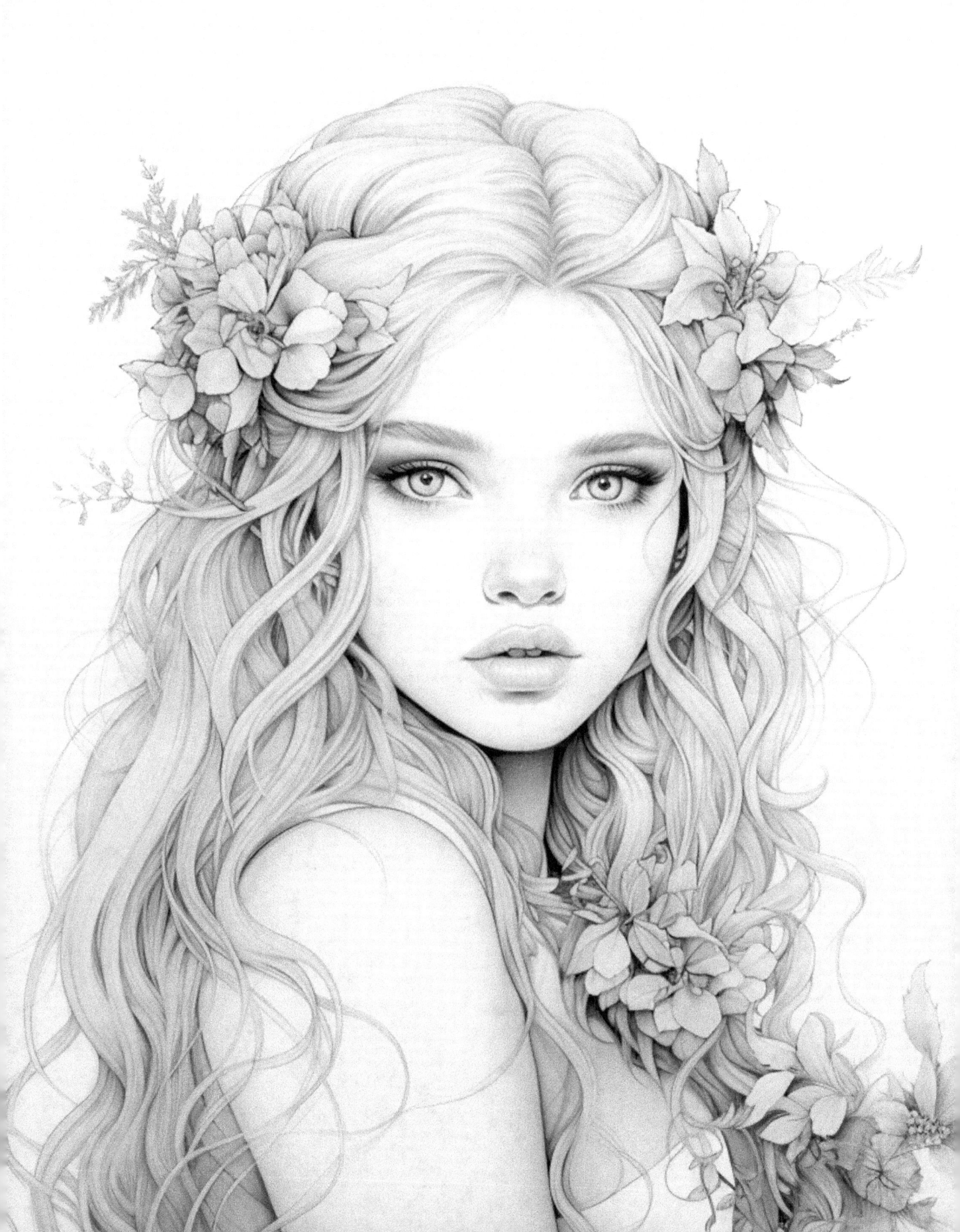

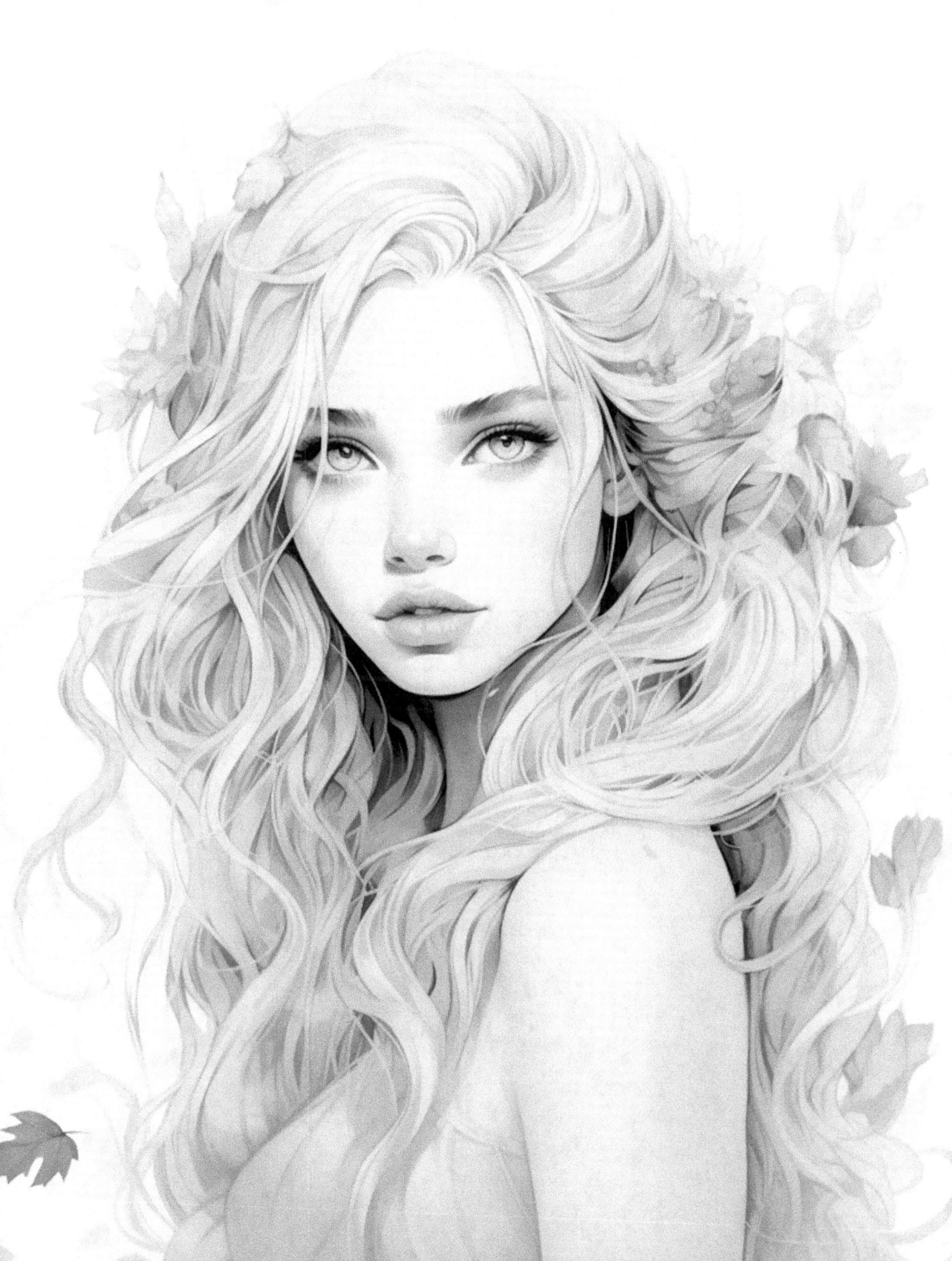

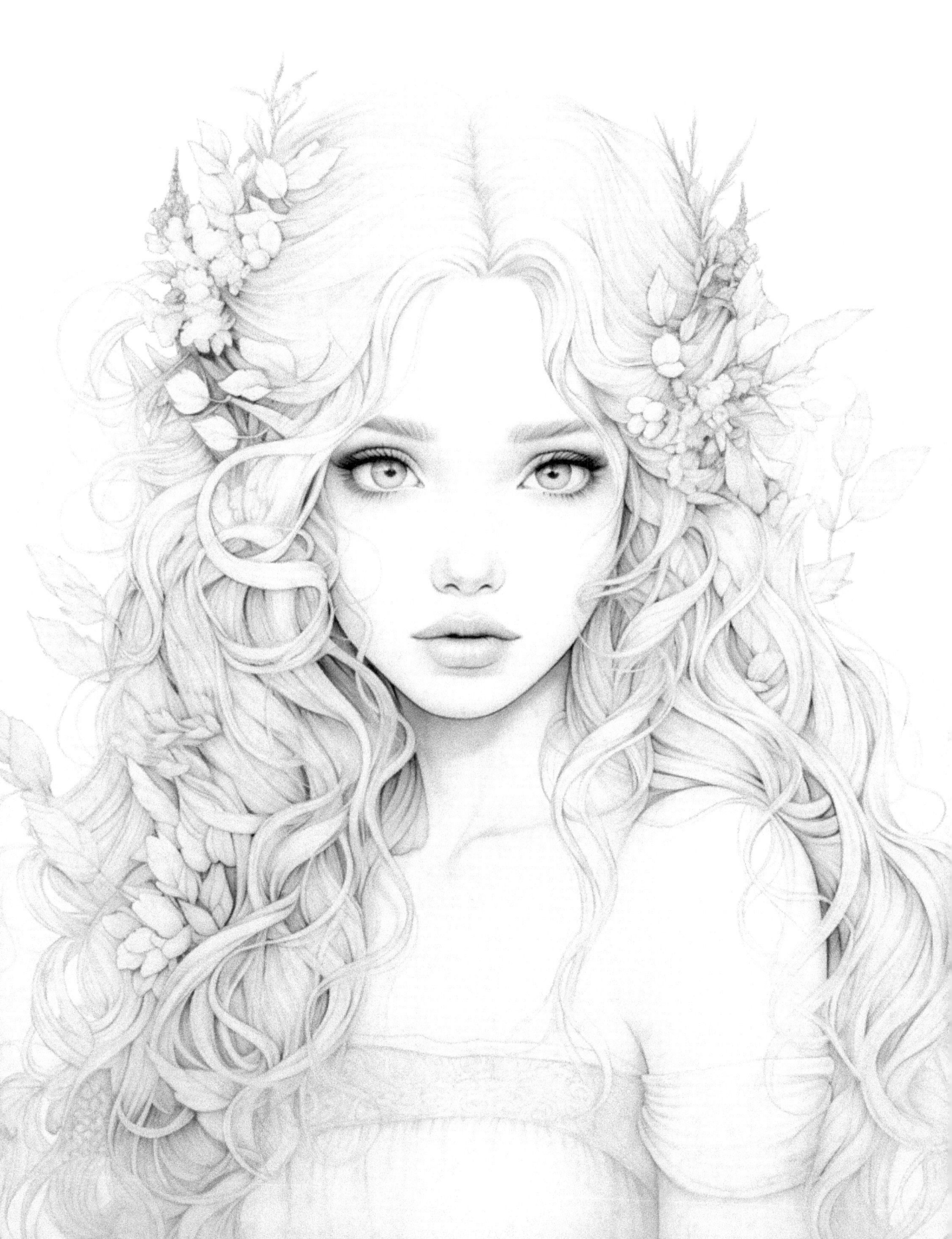

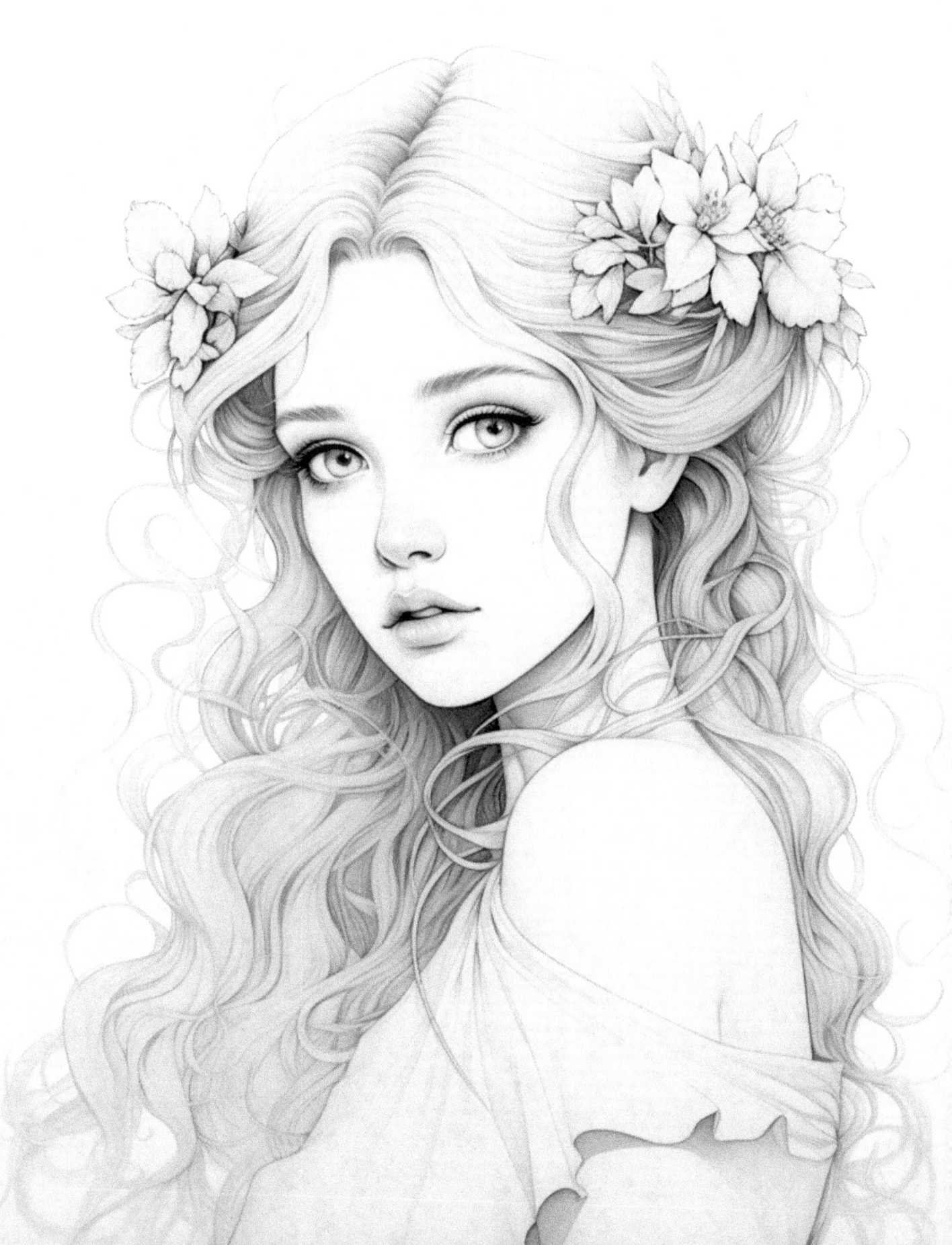

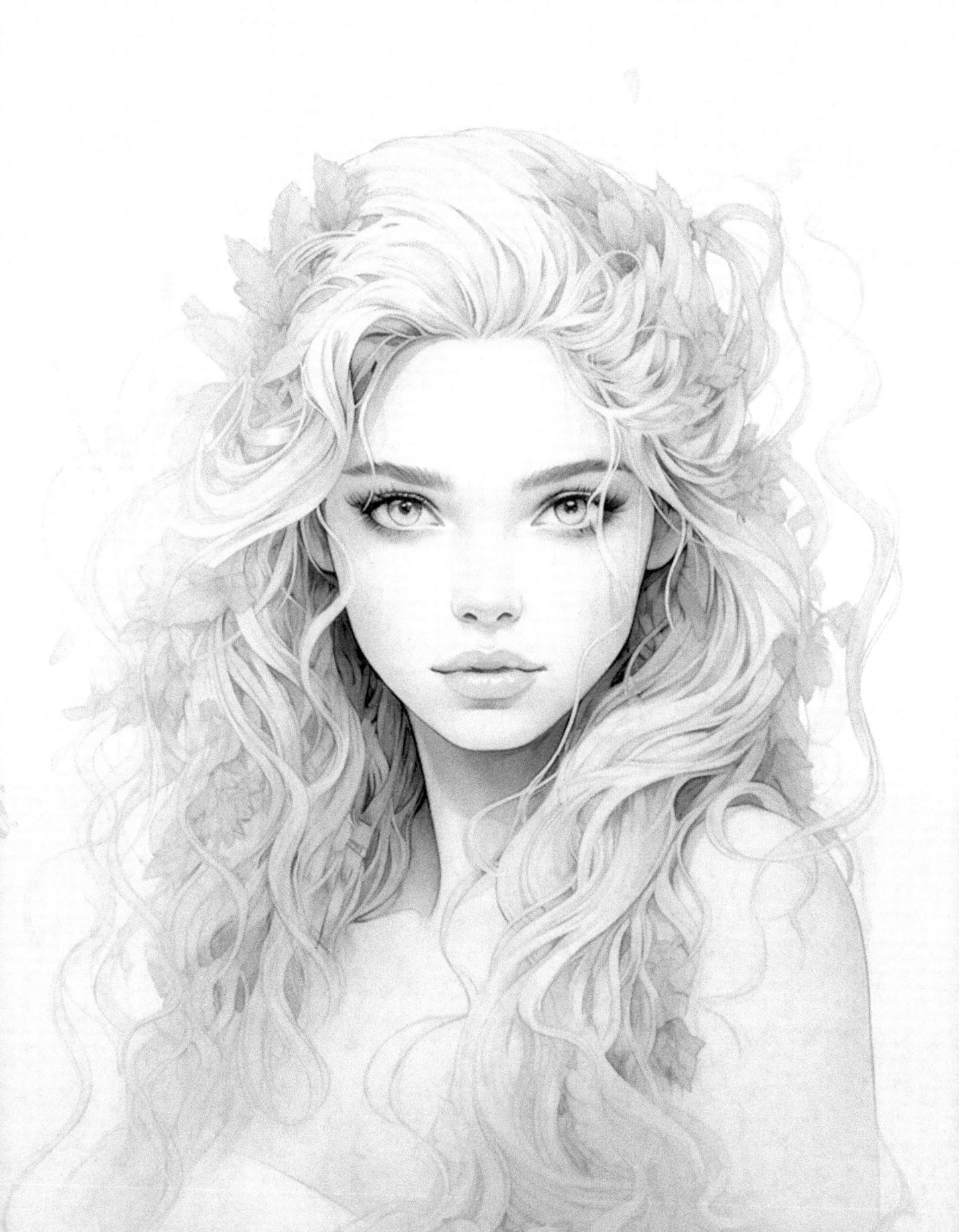

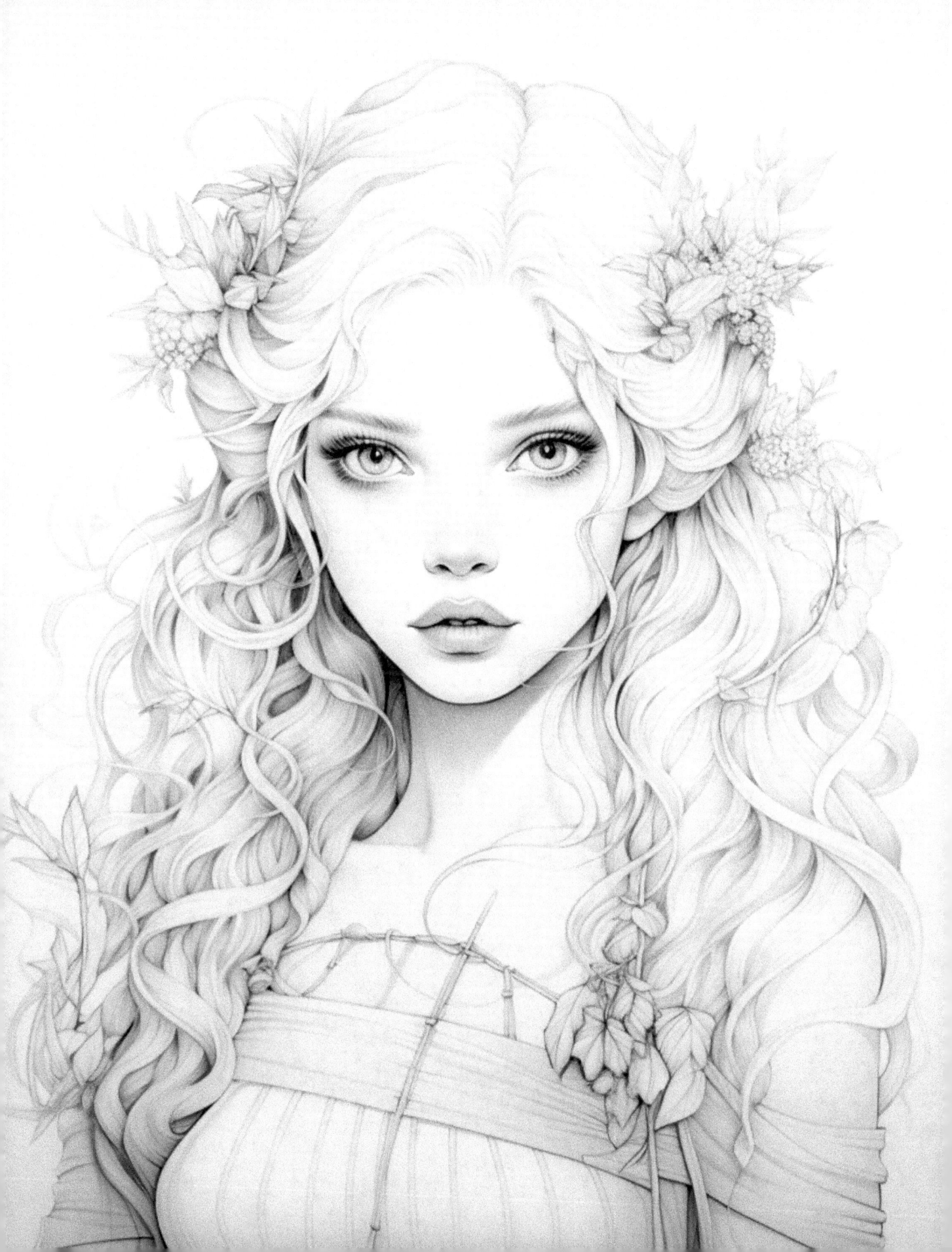

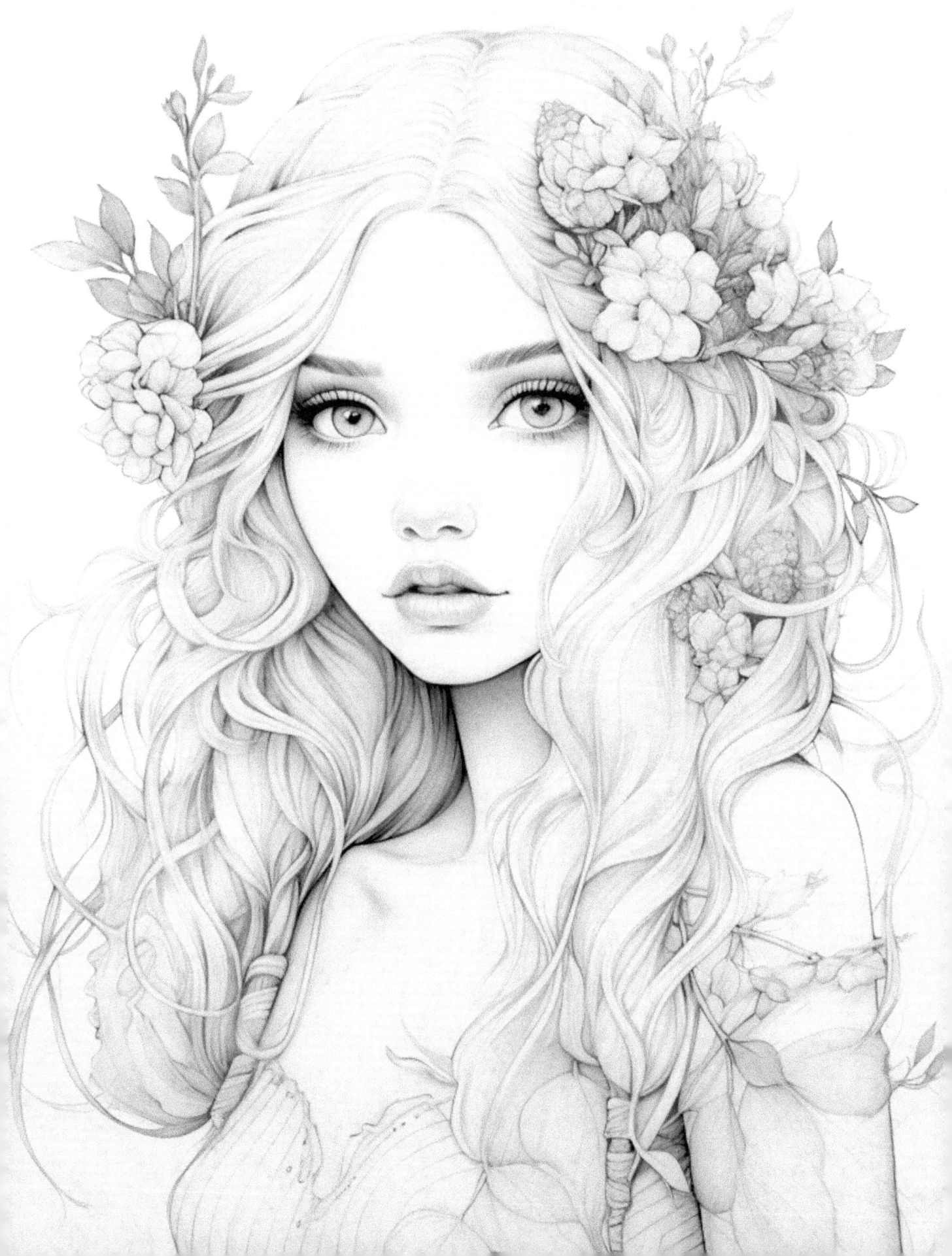

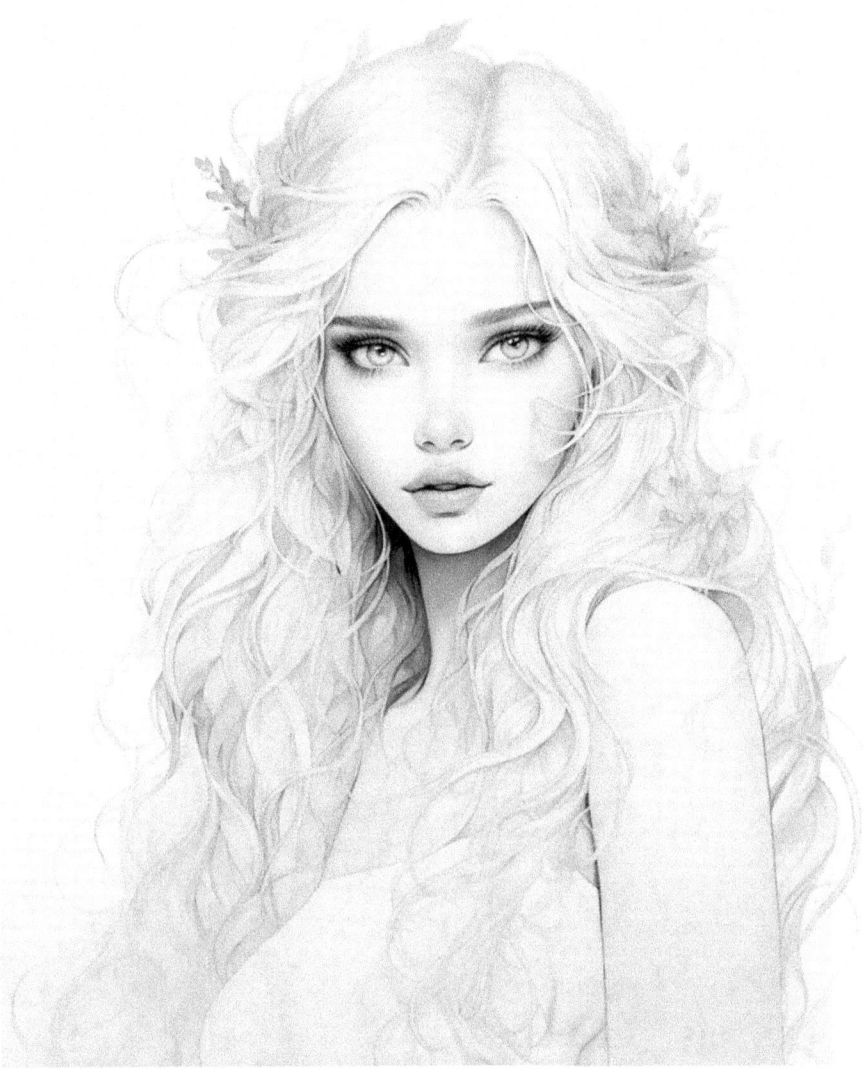

Dear Reader,
Thank you so much for taking the time to explore this coloring book! We hope that it has brought you many moments of joy, relaxation, and creativity. As the author, I would like to express my deepest appreciation for your support and interest in this project. It was a labor of love to create this book, and knowing that it has touched your life in some small way means the world to me. If you enjoyed coloring in these pages, we would be incredibly grateful if you could leave a positive review on Amazon. Your words and feedback will help other readers discover this book and allow us to continue to share our passion for coloring with others. Thank you again for being a part of this journey.

Sincerely, Kristina Lewis

P.S.To stay informed about our products and to get a **free illustration**, write an email to : tinystarscoloring@yahoo.com regard: newsletter